MOUNTAIN BIKE OWNER'S MANUAL

BY **LENNARD ZINN** AND THE
TECHNICAL EDITORS OF
VELONEWS

VELOPRESS ▪ BOULDER, COLORADO

The Mountain Bike Owner's Manual

Copyright © 1998 Inside Communications

International Standard Book Number: 1-884737-52-8

Library of Congress Cataloging-in Publication Data applied for.

Printed in the USA
Distributed in the United States and Canada by Publishers Group West.

1830 North 55th Street
Boulder, Colorado 80301-2700 USA
303/440-0601 Fax 303/444-6788
email: velopress@7dogs.com

To purchase additional copies of this book or other VeloPress books, call
800/234-8356 or visit us on the Web at www.velocatalogue.com.

Table of Contents

	Introduction	1
Chapter 1	Safety and responsibility	7
Chapter 2	Tools	17
Chapter 3	Comfort is key	25
Chapter 4	Emergency repairs	37
Chapter 5	The drive train	47
Chapter 6	Wheels and tires	65
Chapter 7	Brakes	81
Chapter 8	Pedals	93
Chapter 9	Forks and headsets	101
Chapter 10	The stuff at the back of the book	113

To Emily and Sarah

Acknowledgments

Thanks to Amy Sorrells of VeloPress for driving this project along and for working closely with me on content. Charles Pelkey, John Wilcockson and Lori Hobkirk made this book happen by coming up with great ideas and supplying their expert editing. Thanks, Todd Telander, for great illustrations, and Chas Chamberlin and Daisy Bauer for great charts and design work.

Introduction

ABOUT THIS BOOK

This book is useful to anyone who owns a mountain bike. Try to think of it as another tool. It can be easily carried along on rides and extended bike trips to provide handy information when you need it most.

To a rider new to working on bikes, the repair and maintenance information contained within could prevent a lot of agony. Bike disasters, especially those a long way from home, can often be avoided by following the simple maintenance steps and pre-ride checks in this manual. If the bike *does* break down on the trail, being able to fix it and ride home could give many a rider new-found confidence and a feeling of freedom to embark on longer, harder rides. Preparation in terms of

clothing, tools and emergency equipment can provide those same feelings as well. This book contains simple techniques to fix any number of things that can go wrong on the trail. We've also included a bit of advice on how to dress (Function rather than appearance is key here. We offer no advice on baggy shorts, color schemes or even on how to cultivate the perfect goatee.) and what to bring along on rides of varying length and conditions.

The Records section is useful for any mountain bike owner. It provides a single, easily accessible place to keep all information about your bike. The date and place of purchase and serial numbers of all original equipment on the bike can be recorded on lines earmarked for that purpose, as can information

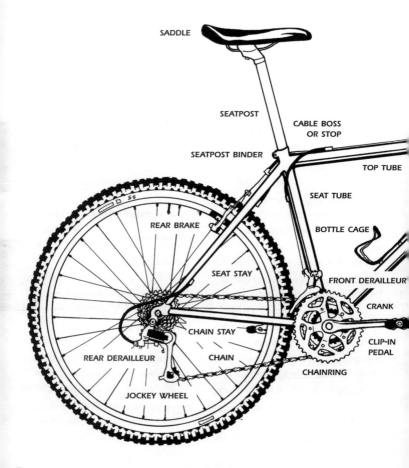

SADDLE

SEATPOST

CABLE BOSS
OR STOP

SEATPOST BINDER

TOP TUBE

SEAT TUBE

REAR BRAKE

BOTTLE CAGE

SEAT STAY

FRONT DERAILLEUR

CRANK

CHAIN STAY

CLIP-IN
PEDAL

REAR DERAILLEUR

CHAIN

CHAINRING

JOCKEY WHEEL

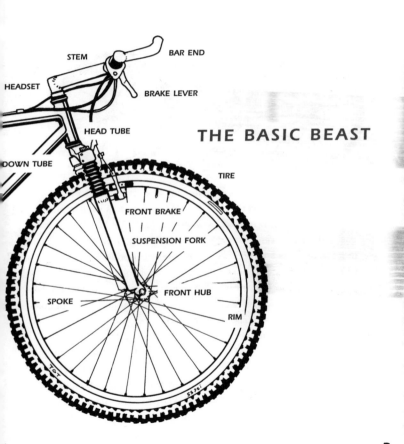

STEM

BAR END

HEADSET

BRAKE LEVER

HEAD TUBE

THE BASIC BEAST

DOWN TUBE

TIRE

FRONT BRAKE

SUSPENSION FORK

FRONT HUB

SPOKE

RIM

RIGID

about any replacement and upgraded parts that have been subsequently installed. The pocket in the back serves as a central place to keep receipts and warranty information. Should you need it, you can get to that information to get warranty service or replacement of defective parts.

Use the distance record to keep track of not only your bike's total mileage, but more importantly, how far it has gone since maintenance was performed. The book also contains information to simplify the calibration of a new computer or how to calibrate your existing computer after you've changed the battery and can't find that little piece of paper with the instructions. The suggested service and regular maintenance schedule provides a simple checklist and reminders for keeping your bike in good running order.

TYPES OF MOUNTAIN BIKES

Among mid- to high-end mountain bikes, the vast majority of bikes sold are front-suspension models (also known as "hardtails"). In other words, the bikes have a rigid frame

with a suspension fork mounted on it. This type of bike gives many of the advantages of suspension without the added weight and complexity of rear suspension. A suspension fork allows a bike to be ridden with more comfort and at much higher speeds over rough ground.

If you've just purchased a bike, this is the time to get into the habit of taking good care of it. Even if you've had one for a while and let it go a little too long without proper care and feeding, you can make amends by following a few simple steps. By clearly spelling out the steps necessary to properly maintain and repair a bicycle, even those who see themselves as having no mechanical skills will be able to tackle problems as they arise. With a little bit of practice and a willingness to learn, your bike will suddenly transform itself from a mysterious black box, too complicated to tamper with, to a simple, very understandable machine that is a delight to work on and more importantly, a joy to ride. Have fun. — LENNARD ZINN AND THE TECHNICAL STAFF OF VELONEWS

Safety and responsibility

"He hath a wisdom that doth guide his valor to act in safety …"
— *THE TRAGEDY OF MACBETH,* WILLIAM SHAKESPEARE, 1606

As we've said, the mountain bike is an amazingly hardy creature. It is capable of taking incredible abuse — much more than either you, your riding companions or folks on the trail. There are a few rules of the (off-)road worth keeping in mind as you begin to explore the possibilities of your new (or old) bike.

HELMETS

Not enough can be said about the value of wearing a helmet. You can still live a long and happy life after breaking almost any other bone in your body other than your skull. It is well worth keeping it intact, and the price you have to pay to protect it is small.

Helmet technology has come a long way in recent years. Helmets are relatively comfortable, light, cool and inexpensive these days, although you can spend a lot of money to get one of the coolest, lightest and most comfortable and adjustable models.

When buying a helmet, make certain it meets the basic ANSI, Snell or ASTM certification tests (there should be a sticker on the inside of the helmet). In order to pass any of these tests, it must provide good head protection against a wide variety of forceful impacts.

Get into the habit of wearing a helmet whenever you ride a bike. If you have children, this is particularly important, so that they always associate riding with putting on a helmet. Wear your helmet even when you are going on little rides up and down the block with them. Later, when they start doing wild things on a bike, you will not be fighting battles to get them to wear their helmet.

Now that you have your head on straight, make sure your bike is in good working order.

PRE-RIDE INSPECTION

1. Check to be sure that the quick-release levers or axle nuts (the ones that secure the hub axle to the dropouts) are tight.
2. Check the brake pads for excessive or uneven wear.
3. Grab and twist the brake pads and brake arms to make sure the bolts are tight.
4. Squeeze the brake levers. This

TIGHTENING QUICK RELEASE

should bring the pads flat against the rims (or slightly toed-in) without hitting the tires. Make certain that you cannot squeeze the levers all of the way to the handlebars.
5. Spin the wheels. Check for wobbles while sighting on the rims, not the tires. (If a tire wobbles excessively on a straight rim, it may not be fully seated in the rim; check it all of the way around on both sides.) Make sure that the rims do not rub on the brake pads.
6. Check the tire pressure. On most mountain bike tires, the proper pressure is between 35 and 60 pounds per square inch (psi).

Look to see that there are no foreign objects sticking in the tire. If there are, you may have to pull the tube out and repair or replace it. For some, it may be worth your time to look at the selection of tire sealants at your local bike shop. This goop is placed inside the tube and fills at least the smaller holes you may get.

7. Check the tires for excessive wear, cracking or gashes.

8. Be certain that the handlebar and stem are tight and that the stem is lined up with the front tire.

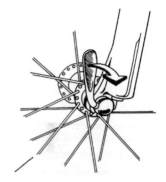

OPENING QUICK RELEASE SKEWER

9. Check that the gears shift smoothly and the chain does not skip or shift by itself. Ensure that indexed (or "click") shifting moves the chain one cog, starting with the first click.

Make sure that the chain does not overshift the smallest or biggest rear cog or the smallest or biggest front chainring.

10. Check the chain for rust, dirt, stiff links or noticeable signs of wear. It should be clean and lubricated. (Be cautious about overdoing it, though. Over-lubricated,

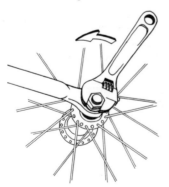

LOOSENING AXLE NUT

gooey chains pick up a lot of dirt, particularly in dry climates.) The chain should be replaced on a mountain bike about every 500 to 1000 miles of off-road riding or every 2000 miles of paved riding.
11. Apply the front brake and push the bike forward and back. The headset should be tight and make no "clunking" noises or allow the fork any fore-aft play.

Finally, you need to get into the habit of regularly checking your suspension fork for wear and tear.

FORK INSPECTION

For the most part, forks are pretty durable, but they do break sometimes. A fork failure can ruin your day, since the means of control of the bike is eliminated. Such loss of control usually involves the rapid transfer of your body directly onto the ground resulting in substantial pain and serious injury.

When you inspect a fork, remove the front wheel, clean the mud off, and look under the crown and between the fork legs.

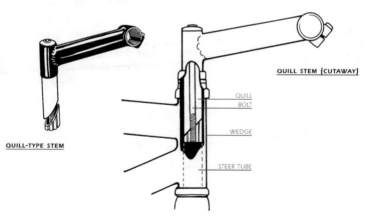

QUILL STEM (CUTAWAY)

QUILL
BOLT

WEDGE

STEER TUBE

QUILL-TYPE STEM

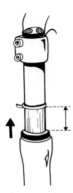

Carefully examine all of the outside areas. Look for any areas where the paint or finish looks cracked or stretched. Look for bent parts, from little ripples in fork legs to skewed cantilever posts and bent dropouts.

Put your wheel back in, and watch to see if the fork legs twist when you tighten the hub into the dropouts. Check to make sure that a true wheel centers under the fork crown. If it doesn't, turn the wheel around and put it back in the fork. That way you can confirm whether the misalignment is in the fork or the wheel. If the wheel lines up off to one side when it is in one way and off the same amount to the other side when it is in the other way, the wheel is off, and the fork is straight. If the wheel is skewed off to the same side in the fork no matter which direction you place the wheel, the fork is misaligned.

Hold the stem up next to the steering tube to make sure that, when your stem is inserted to the depth you have been using it, the bottom of the stem is always more than an inch below the bottom of the steering tube threads. If you expand your stem in the threaded region, you are asking for trouble; the threads cut the steering tube wall thickness down by about 50 percent, and each thread offers a sharp breakage plane along which the tube can cleave.

ON TELESCOPING SUSPENSION FORKS

Check that any clamp bolts are tight (ideally, you would do this with a torque wrench to check that they are tightened to the torque recommended by the fork manufacturer). If you have titanium clamp bolts on your fork crown and you do lots of fast and rough downhill riding, consider replacing them annually; the heads of titanium fork crown bolts have been known to snap off. Check for oil leaks, either from around the top of the outer leg or around the bolt at the bottom of the outer leg. Check for torn, cracked or missing seals around the top of the outer leg.

On linkage forks, there are a lot of bolts, pins and pivots that need to be checked regularly. Make sure that all bolts are tight and all pins have their circlips or other retaining devices in place so they do not fall out. Check for cracks and bends around the pivot points.

If you have any doubts about anything on your fork, take it to

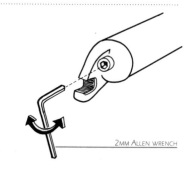

2MM ALLEN WRENCH

ADJUSTING DAMPING ON ROCK SHOX JUDY FORK

the expert at your bike shop. When it comes to forks, err on the side of caution. Replacing a damaged fork is expensive, but it is probably a lot cheaper than not replacing it.

FRAME INSPECTION

You can avoid potentially dangerous, or at least ride-shortening frame failures by inspecting your frame frequently. If you find damage, and you are not sure how dangerous the bike is to ride, take it to a bike shop for advice.

1. Clean your frame every few rides, so that you can spot problems early.

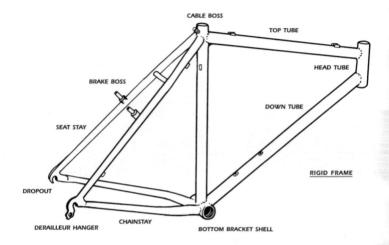

CABLE BOSS

TOP TUBE

HEAD TUBE

BRAKE BOSS

DOWN TUBE

SEAT STAY

RIGID FRAME

DROPOUT

DERAILLEUR HANGER   CHAINSTAY   BOTTOM BRACKET SHELL

2. Inspect all tubes for cracks, bends, buckles, dents, and paint stretching or cracking, especially near the joints where stress is at its highest. If in doubt, take it to an expert for advice.

3. Inspect the rear dropouts and the welds around the brake bosses and cable hanger for cracks. Check to be sure the dropouts, brake bosses and cable hangers are not bent. Some dropouts and brake bosses bolt on (or, in some cases, even glue on) and are replaceable. Otherwise, badly bent or broken dropouts, brake bosses and cable hangers need to be replaced; a framebuilder in your area may be able to do it.

4. Look for deeply rusted areas on steel frames. Remove the seatpost every few months and invert the bike to see if water pours out of the seat tube. Look and feel for deep

rusted areas inside. We recommend shooting rust-preventive sprays for bicycle frames, WD-40 or oil inside your tubes periodically. Remember to grease both the seatpost and inside of the seat tube when you reinsert the seatpost.

5. On suspension frames, disconnect the shock. Move the swingarm up and down, and flex it laterally, feeling for play or binding in the pivots. Check the shock for leaking oil, cracks, a bent shaft or other damage.

6. Check that a true and properly dished wheel sits straight in the frame, centered between the chainstays and seatstays, and lined up in the same plane as the front triangle. Tightening the hub skewer should not result in chainstay or seatstay bowing or twisting.

TRAIL SAFETY

Mountain biking in the backcountry can be dangerous. A rash of deaths and injuries in the mid-1990s underscores the need to prepare properly and to take personal responsibility for your own and others' safety when riding in deserted country.

We all tend to believe that disasters only happen to other people, but the risk is always there, so be careful. This shouldn't discourage you from riding in the backcountry. It should encourage you to think and utilize the following 12 basic backcountry survival skills, they could make the difference between life and death.

1. Always take plenty of water. You can survive a long time without food, but not without water.

2. Tell someone where you are going and when you expect to return. If you know of someone who is missing, call the police or sheriff.

3. If you find personal effects on the ground, assume it could indicate that someone is lost or in trouble. Report the find and mark the location.

4. If you get lost, backtrack. Even if going back is longer, it is better

than getting stranded.

5. Don't go down something you can't get back up.

6. Bring matches, extra clothing and food, and perhaps a flashlight and an aluminized emergency blanket, in case you have to spend the night out or need to signal searchers.

7. If the area is new to you, go with someone who is familiar with it, or take a map and compass, and know how to use them.

8. Wear a helmet. It's hard to ride home with a cracked skull.

9. Bring basic first aid and bike tools, and know how to use them well enough to keep yourself and your bike going.

10. Walk your bike when it's appropriate. Falling off a cliff is a poor alternative to taking a few extra seconds or displaying less bravado. Try riding difficult sections to improve your bike handling, but if the exposure is great or a mistake leaves you injured a long way from help, find another place to practice those moves.

11. Don't ride beyond your limits if you are a long way out. Take a break. Get out of the hot sun. Avoid dehydration and bonk by drinking and eating enough.

12. Teach your friends all these things.

Keep in mind that your decisions not only affect you, but they could also affect your riding partners and countless others. Realize that endangering yourself can also endanger the person trying to rescue you. Search and rescue parties are usually made up of helpful people, who will gladly come and save you, but no one appreciates being put in harm's way unnecessarily.

In summary, make appropriate decisions when cycling the back country. Learn survival skills, and prepare well. Recognize that, just because you have a $4000 bike and are riding on popular trails, you are not immune to danger. When ignorance makes us oblivious to danger, it sadly becomes the danger itself.

Tools

CHAPTER 2

"Every tool carries with it the spirit by which it has been created."
— *"Physics and Philosophy," Werner Karl Heisenberg, 1958*

If you plan to work on your bike, for a small investment, you can assemble a reasonable set of tools to accomplish most tasks. As your interests and talents expand, go ahead and add to the collection. No matter what, you should at least assemble a minimal set of tools for trailside repairs.

TRAILSIDE TOOLS
FOR MOST TYPES OF RIDING

You can pack all of this stuff in a bag under your seat, though some prefer to keep the tool kit in a hydration pack (a.k.a. Camelbak) or a fanny pack. The operative words here are light and serviceable. Many of these tools are combined into some of the popular "multi-tools." Make sure you try all the tools at home before relying on them in a crisis.

- Spare tube. This is a no-brainer. Make sure the valve matches the ones on your bike.
- Tire pump or CO_2 cartridge. The bigger the better. Mini-pumps are okay, but they're slow. Make sure the pump is set up for your type of valves.
- At least two plastic tire levers, preferably three.
- Patch kit. You'll need something after you've used your spare tube. Check it every few months to make sure the glue is not dried up.
- Chain tool. Get a light one that works.

17

• Spare chain links from your chain. If you're using a Shimano chain, bring at least two "subpin" rivets.

• Small screwdriver for adjusting derailleurs and other parts.

• Compact set of Allen wrenches that includes 2.5mm, 3mm, 4mm, 5mm and 6mm sizes. (Some of you might need to bring along an 8mm, too.)

• 8mm and 10 mm open-end wrenches.

• Properly sized spoke wrench.

• Matches because you never know when you can be stranded overnight.

• Identification.

• Cash for food, phone calls and to boot side-wall cuts in tires.

FOR LONG OR MULTI-DAY TRIPS

• Spare spokes. Innovations in Cycling sells a really cool folding spoke made from Kevlar. It's worth getting one or two for emergency repairs on a long ride.

• Small plastic bottle of chain lube.

• Small tube of grease.

• Compact 15mm pedal wrench. Be sure to get one with a headset wrench on the other end.

• More money, or its plastic equivalent, which can get you out of lots of scrapes.

TOOLS TO TAKE ON ALL RIDES

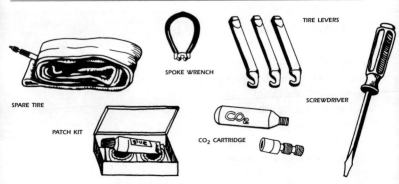

TIRE LEVERS

SPOKE WRENCH

SCREWDRIVER

SPARE TIRE

PATCH KIT

CO2 CARTRIDGE

- A lightweight aluminized folding emergency blanket.
- Rain gear.

You should, of course, also carry proper amounts of food, water and spare clothes.

THE BASIC TOOLS FOR THE SIMPLEST OF JOBS AT HOME

These repairs are the simplest and do not require a workshop, although it is nice to have a good space to work. You will need the following tools:

- Tire pump with a gauge and a valve head to match your tubes.
- Standard screwdrivers: one small, medium and large.
- Phillips-head screwdrivers: one small and one medium.
- Set of three plastic tire levers.
- At least two spare tubes of the same size and valve type as those on your bike.
- Container of regular baby powder. It works well for coating tubes and the inner casings of tires. Do not inhale this stuff; it's bad for the lungs
- Patch kit. Choose one that comes with sandpaper instead of a metal scratcher. At least every 18 months, check that the glue has not dried up, whether open or not.

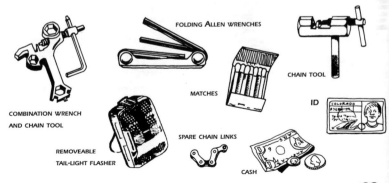

COMBINATION WRENCH
AND CHAIN TOOL

FOLDING ALLEN WRENCHES

MATCHES

CHAIN TOOL

REMOVEABLE
TAIL-LIGHT FLASHER

SPARE CHAIN LINKS

CASH

ID

COMPACT HEADSET AND PEDAL TOOL

KEVLAR SPOKE

GREASE

CHAIN LUBE

RAIN GEAR

EMERGENCY BLANKET

CASH

SPOKE WRENCH

SPARE SPOKE

- One 6-inch adjustable wrench (a.k.a., "Crescent wrench").
- Pliers: regular and needle-nose.
- Set of metric Allen wrenches (or hex keys) that includes 2.5mm, 3mm, 4mm, 5mm, 6mm and 8mm sizes. Folding sets are available and work nicely to keep your wrenches organized. We also recommend buying extras of the 4mm, 5mm and 6mm sizes.
- Set of metric open-end wrenches that includes 7mm, 8mm, 9mm, 10mm, 13mm, 14mm, 15mm and 17mm sizes.
- 15mm pedal wrench. This is thinner and longer than a standard 15mm wrench, but thicker than a cone wrench.
- Chain tool for breaking and reassembling chains.
- Spoke wrench to match the size of nipples used on your wheels.
- Tube or jar of grease. We recommend using grease designed specifically for bicycles; however, standard automotive grease is okay.
- Drip bottle or can of chain lubricant. Please choose a non-aerosol; it is easier to control, uses less packaging, and

wastes less in overspray.

- Rubbing alcohol for removing and installing handlebar grips.
- A lot of rags!

OTHER:

- Most air/oil suspension forks and rear shocks come with a small air pump equipped with the appropriate head and gauge. If you have such a system, the pump needs to be part of your basic tool set.

MORE ELABORATE, BIKE-SPECIFIC TOOLS

Some repairs are a bit more complex, and we recommend that you use a well-organized work space with a shop bench. Keeping your work-space well organized is probably the best way to make maintenance and repair easy and quick. You will need the basics, plus the following tools:

- Portable bike stand. Be sure that the stand is sturdy enough to remain stable when you're really cranking on the wrenches.
- Shop apron (this is to keep your nice duds nice).
- Hacksaw with a fine-toothed blade.

- Set of razor blades or a sharp shop knife.
- Files: one round and one flat.
- Cable cutter for cutting brake and shifter cables without fraying the ends.
- Cable-housing cutter for cutting coaxial-indexed cable housing. If you purchase a Shimano, Park or Wrench Force housing cutter, you won't need to buy a separate cable cutter, since either of these cleanly cuts both cables and housings.
- Set of metric socket wrenches that includes 7mm, 8mm, 9mm, 10mm, 13mm, 14mm and 15mm sizes.
- Crank puller for removing crank arms.
- Medium ball-peen hammer.
- Two headset wrenches. Be sure to check the size of your headset before buying these. This purchase is unnecessary if you have a threadless headset and plan only to work on your own bike.
- Medium bench vise.
- Cassette cog lockring tool for removing cogs from the rear hub.
- Chain whip for holding cogs while loosening the cassette lockring.
- Bottom bracket tools. For Shimano

cartridge bottom brackets or other brands with splined cups, you'll need the splined tool for this type of bottom bracket. For cup-and-one bottom brackets, you'll need a lockring spanner and a pin spanner to fit your bottom bracket.

• Channel-lock pliers.

• Splined pedal spindle removal tool.
• Tube of silicone-based grease if you have Grip Shift and other non-lithium grease for suspension forks.
• One stereo with good tunes. This is especially important if you plan on spending a lot of time working on your bike.

BASIC TOOL KIT FOR THE HOME SHOP

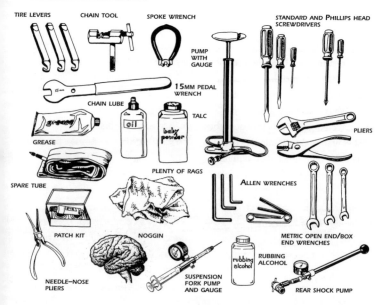

TIRE LEVERS   CHAIN TOOL   SPOKE WRENCH

STANDARD AND PHILLIPS HEAD SCREWDRIVERS

PUMP WITH GAUGE

15MM PEDAL WRENCH

CHAIN LUBE

GREASE

TALC

PLIERS

SPARE TUBE

PLENTY OF RAGS

ALLEN WRENCHES

PATCH KIT

NOGGIN

METRIC OPEN END/BOX END WRENCHES

NEEDLE–NOSE PLIERS

SUSPENSION FORK PUMP AND GAUGE

RUBBING ALCOHOL

REAR SHOCK PUMP

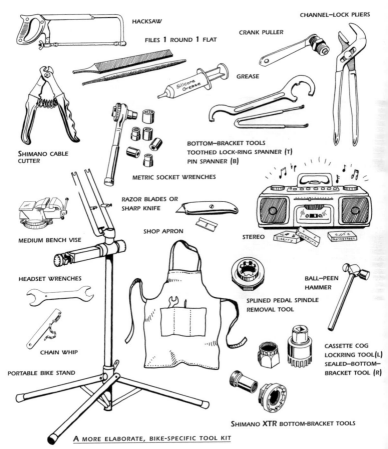

HACKSAW

FILES 1 ROUND 1 FLAT

CRANK PULLER

CHANNEL–LOCK PLIERS

GREASE

Silicone Grease

SHIMANO CABLE CUTTER

BOTTOM–BRACKET TOOLS
TOOTHED LOCK-RING SPANNER (T)
PIN SPANNER (B)

METRIC SOCKET WRENCHES

RAZOR BLADES OR SHARP KNIFE

SHOP APRON

STEREO

MEDIUM BENCH VISE

HEADSET WRENCHES

SPLINED PEDAL SPINDLE REMOVAL TOOL

BALL–PEEN HAMMER

CHAIN WHIP

PORTABLE BIKE STAND

CASSETTE COG LOCKRING TOOL(L)
SEALED–BOTTOM–BRACKET TOOL (R)

SHIMANO XTR BOTTOM-BRACKET TOOLS

A MORE ELABORATE, BIKE-SPECIFIC TOOL KIT

Comfort is key

"For I feel so set up and comfortable as niver was..."
— "SILAS MARNER," GEORGE ELIOT, 1861

FIT IS FUNCTION

Let's assume that you now have a bike with a properly sized frame. But it is important to remember that frame fit is only part of the equation. Except for the standover clearance, a good frame fit is relatively meaningless if the seat setback, seat height, handlebar height and handlebar reach are not set correctly for you. So let's make sure that your bike fits your body like it was made for you.

<u>FINDING THE RIGHT SADDLE HEIGHT</u>

WITH A RIGID SEATPOST

When your foot is at the bottom of the stroke, lock your knee without rocking your hips. Do this sitting on your bike on a trainer with someone else observing. Your foot should be level, or the heel should be slightly higher than the ball of the foot. Another way to determine seat height is to measure your inseam measurement – the distance from your crotch to the floor – and multiply it by 1.09. That should be the length from the center of the pedal spindle (when the pedal is down) to one of the points on the top of the saddle where your butt bones (ischial tuberosities) contact it. Adjust the seat height until you get it the proper height.

NOTE: If you do a lot of technical riding and descending, you may wish to have a lower saddle for better bike-handling control.

WITH A SUSPENSION SEATPOST

The riding position you are trying to achieve with a suspension
seatpost is the same as with a rigid
seatpost. The problem is that measurement of the seat height without
the rider sitting on the saddle will
not give the measurement that
exists while actually riding. There
are a number of ways to deal with
this problem.

One approach is to measure the
amount the seatpost compresses
when the rider sits on it, add this
length to the seat height you calculated in the section above, and set
the seat there. You measure the
amount of seatpost travel that is
used up when you sit on the bike by
measuring the distance, with the
rider on and off the seat, from a ref-
erence point at the head of the post
to the top of the seat tube.

Another method is to measure the
distance from the bottom bracket to
the seat rails when the seat height is
set to the measurement calculated in
the section above. Have someone
else take that same measurement
while you are sitting on the seat.
Raise the seatpost the difference
between these two measurements to
end up with the correct seat height
while you are actually riding.

Yet another method is to adjust
the seat height so that an observer
can see that your foot is level when
it is at the bottom of the stroke when
your knee is locked.

SADDLE SETBACK

Sit on your bike on a stationary
trainer with your cranks in a horizontal position. Keep your foot at the
angle it is at that point when pedaling. Have a friend drop a plumb line
from the front of your knee below
your knee cap. You can use a heavy
ring or washer tied to a string for the
plumb line. The plumb line should
bisect the pedal axle or pass up to
2cm behind it (you will need to lean
the knee out to get the string to hang
clear). A saddle centered in this manner encourages smooth pedaling at

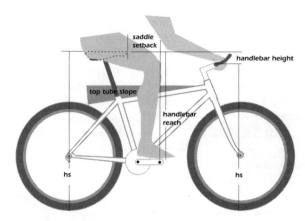

Diagram labels: saddle setback, handlebar height, top tube slope, handlebar reach, hs, hs

high RPMs, while 2cm behind the pedal spindle encourages powerful seated climbing.

Slide the saddle back and forth on the seatpost, until you achieve the desired fore-aft saddle position. Set the saddle level or very close to it. Re-check the seat height as outlined above, since fore-aft saddle movements affect seat-to-pedal distance as well.

HANDLEBAR POSITION

Measure the handlebar height relative to the saddle height by measuring the vertical distance of the saddle and bar up from the floor. How much higher the saddle is than your bar (or vice versa) depends on your flexibility, riding style, overall size, and type of riding you prefer.

Aggressive and tall cross-country riders will prefer to have their saddle 10cm or more higher than the bars. Shorter riders will want proportionately less drop, as will less aggressive riders. Riders doing lots of downhills will want their bars higher; downhill racers often have

2cm to 4cm of drop from bar to saddle, and mountain bike slalom riders' bars are usually much higher than their saddles. Generally, people beginning mountain-bike riding will like their bars high and can lower them as they become more comfortable with the bike, with going fast, and with riding more technical terrain.

If in doubt, start with 4cm of drop and vary it from there. The higher the bar, the greater the tendency is for the front wheel to pull up off of the ground when climbing, and the more wind resistance you can expect. Change the bar height by raising or lowering the stem, or by switching stems and/or bars.

SETTING HANDLEBAR REACH

The reach from the saddle to the handlebar is also very dependent on personal preference. More aggressive riders will want a more stretched-out position than will casual riders. This is a pretty subjective area and depends on a rider's own perception of comfort and efficiency. It is

worth experimenting.

A useful starting place is to drop a plumb line from the back of your elbow with your arms bent in a comfortable riding position. This plane determined by your elbows and the plumb line should be 2cm to 4cm horizontally ahead of each knee at the point in the pedal stroke when the crank arm is horizontal forward. The idea is to select a position you find comfortable and efficient; listen to what your body wants.

Vary the saddle-bar distance by changing stem length, not by changing the seat fore-aft position, which would affect pedaling efficiency. **Note:** There is no single formula for determining handlebar reach and height. We can tell you that the common method of placing your elbow against the saddle and seeing if your fingertips reach the handlebar is close to useless. Similarly, the often suggested method of seeing if the handlebar obscures your vision of the front hub is not worth the brief time it takes to look, being dependent on elbow bend and front end geometry. Another method involving dropping a plumb bob from the rider's nose is dependent on the handlebar height and elbow bend and thus does not lend itself to a proscribed relationship for all riders … especially for those of us with long noses!

BAR ENDS

Bar ends are not a necessity, but many riders prefer them.

With most bar ends, installation is about as straightforward as can be. You will need to move the grips, brake levers and shift levers inboard on the bars enough that there is room for the bar ends to clamp at the ends of the bar. Usually, all you need to do is loosen the clamp bolt on the bar end with a 5mm hex key, slide the bar end onto the bar until it protrudes out of the other side of the bar end's clamp, and tighten the bolt down.

Some bar ends use a different bolt size, and some have different clamping mechanisms. Consult the bar end owner's manual if it is not obvious how to install them.

When clamping bar ends to superlight handlebars or carbon-fiber bars, extra care must be taken to avoid ruining the bar. Some lightweight bars come with small sleeves you insert in the ends of the bar for support under the bar end clamps.

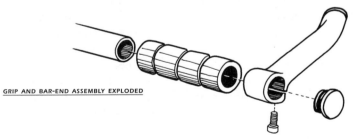

GRIP AND BAR-END ASSEMBLY EXPLODED

BAR-END ANGLE FOR PERFORMANCE RIDERS

15 DEGREES

BAR-END ANGLE FOR CASUAL RIDERS

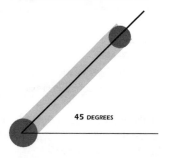

45 DEGREES

Others have a marked-off section where clamping a bar end is acceptable, so cutting off this section and then installing bar ends is a no-no. With lightweight and carbon-fiber bars, a wider bar-end clamp that closes cylindrically symmetrically will damage the bar less than a narrow clamp or one that ovalizes the

bar as it tightens down. If you see significant ovalization happening or hear cracking noises, stop tightening the bolt and consult a knowledgeable shop mechanic.

BAR-END POSITION

The bar ends should be set up in the range between horizontal and pointed up 15 degrees. Find the position you find comfortable for pulling while climbing standing or seated, and for pedaling while seated for long stretches on paved roads.

NOTE: Do not use the bar ends to raise your hand position by pointing them vertically up. If you want a higher hand position, get a taller or more up-angled stem, and/or a higher-rise handlebar. Bar ends are not meant to be stood straight up and held on to for cruising along sitting up high; that is the mountain bike equivalent of flipping a road drop bar upside down to lift the hands. As with the road bar equivalent, you cannot reach the brakes when you need them.

GRIPS

Grips are necessary to offer a good hold on the bars, increase comfort, and to increase the diameter you are holding onto a size that is amenable to your hands. Pick grips that are a diameter, shape and softness you like. You will need shorter grips if you are using twist shifters than if you have shift levers. Grips can be cut to length with scissors.

Install grips by sliding them onto the bars with rubbing alcohol on the bar and inside the grips. Water also works, but rubbing alcohol evaporates

GROOVE PRE-MARKED ON GRIP

TRIMMING GRIP TO ACCOMMODATE BAR END

USING WATER TO REMOVE GRIP

faster. Some folks use citrus-based degreasers and certain spray adhesives. One thing you do not want is for your grips to slip around while you are riding. A grip can be secured tightly to the bars by wrapping a piece or two of thin wire around it and twisting it tightly in place with pliers. Clip the twisted end and bend it over so it does not gouge your hand.

CLOTHING

There are good reasons for riding in clothing made specifically for mountain biking. Your comfort, enjoyment and even health are usually enhanced by using clothing designed for your specific application.

HELMETS, HELMETS, HELMETS ...YES, YOU DO NEED ONE

We already mentioned the importance of wearing a helmet, but it doesn't hurt to mention it again. There are compelling reasons to wear one. The odds are pretty good that you have – or will have – a job that involves the use of your brain at least at some point during an eight-hour day. If so, you should view the wearing of a bicycle helmet as a form of career insurance if nothing else. A bicycle helmet will also go a long way toward protecting that charming, sharp and witty personality you have spent so many years developing.

Don't scrimp! Don't buy a $10 helmet unless you have a $10 head.

Shoes

Mountain-bike shoes are essential for comfort, enjoyment and efficiency. The stiff soles distribute pedaling forces over your entire foot and avoid the "hot spots" that can be caused by a concentration of pressure under the ball of the foot from a flexible shoe mushing over the pedal. A shoe with cleat-mounting holes can be equipped with cleats to take advantage of the greater pedaling efficiency and safety of clip-in pedals.

Velcro straps and ratcheting buckles may replace laces or can be used in combination with laces. They offer more security than laces alone and serve to cover the laces as well, preventing them from getting caught in the chainrings.

The aggressive treads on mountain-bike shoes combined with a recessed cleat allow you to walk and run comfortably and efficiently over a variety of terrain. For getting traction in mud, some shoes also offer threaded holes for screw-on spikes.

Shorts and Jerseys

Cycling shorts can save your butt on a long or rough ride. They are padded for obvious reasons, and the stretchy, tight-fitting material is designed to move with you as you pedal. They usually have some sort of chamois or synthetic chamois pad in the crotch. They are meant to be worn without underwear to prevent dry chafing and wrinkling of the extra layer.

When you negotiate technical terrain, tight-fitting shorts allow you to slide off of the back or front of the saddle and back on again without catching loose fabric on the saddle. Stretch shorts also allow you to put on extra layers when it gets cold without bunching up underneath. Bib shorts (those with integrated Lycra suspenders) will stay up and will not constrict you around your waist, since they do not have a waistband.

A cycling jersey will have pockets in the back to carry extra stuff such as food, clothes and tools. It also will have a zipper in front, sometimes even a full-length zipper, which is useful for adjusting to changes in temperature. Cycling jerseys are made out of a variety of fabrics for different conditions.

GLOVES

Gloves protect your hands from jarring and abrasion. At a minimum, you want standard, fingerless cycling gloves to protect the heels of your hands.

Continuous shock to the hands without gloves (and well-padded grips) leads to fatigue and can even result in carpal-tunnel syndrome after many years.

Riding at the edge of your ability on technical trails can cause you to fall fairly frequently. Since the most natural reaction is to try and break your fall with your hands, it is a good idea to protect them. Full-finger gloves are a good idea for mountain biking to prevent your fingers from getting cut or your fingernails from getting torn when falling.

When using twist shifters, gloves that are reinforced in the thumb and forefinger area (even having a full thumb and forefinger) can prevent blisters and calluses from appearing in that area.

SUNGLASSES

Good sunglasses prevent ultraviolet rays from damaging your eyes. They also do a pretty good job of keeping bugs and dirt out. Shielding your eyes from the wind also helps keep them from drying out.

Along these lines, sunscreen on exposed areas of your skin is not a bad idea on long rides.

COLD-WEATHER CLOTHING

In cold weather, proper clothing is important for your comfort as well as your health.

In rain or snow, you need water-proof clothing, preferably breathable, like GoreTex. If you will be out in wet weather for a couple of hours or more, a waterproof jacket and pants as well as waterproof shoe covers and helmet cover should be considered to be necessities. A couple of clip-on fenders will also be useful.

In cold weather, you want to wear enough clothing to stay warm, keeping in mind that at times you will be moving fast without pedaling to stay warm, so the amount of clothes that you would wear for walking, snowshoeing or cross-country skiing will be insufficient. Furthermore, wear layers of clothing so that you can adjust your surface temperature as your body or the air warms up or cools down by removing or putting on layers.

APPROPRIATE GEAR IS A NECESSITY

Proper "technical fabrics" are preferable to cotton and even wool for cycling in cold weather. These fabrics are designed to wick moisture *away* from your skin and transport the water droplets to the surface layers to evaporate. Cotton will tend to get wet and clammy as you sweat and can result in your getting very cold. Wool still has insulating ability when wet, but it will still not be as good as dry layers. Wool will also absorb a lot of water and get heavy, and, besides, properly washing wool garments is a pain.

To protect yourself from the wind – especially your chest – you want windproof layers. A wind jacket or vest is great to have, as is a jersey with Windstopper fabric in front. A newspaper or piece of synthetic chamois can be slid under some of your layers to keep wind off of your chest.

Insulated shoe covers, warm gloves and a warm hat or earmuffs are important. On a bike, your extremities are exposed and moving quickly through the air and can get very cold.

Whenever you head out on a ride, wear appropriate clothing for the weather conditions at that time, and prepare for conditions that you might encounter later. This is particularly important on long rides in the mountains, since weather in the mountains is notoriously fickle, particularly if you are out long enough to give it time to change dramatically. I recommend bringing

at least a windproof vest, a chamois bib or a folded-up piece of newspaper, some thin gloves and a hat, headband, or earmuffs. Rain gear should also be carried along if clouds are threatening.

HYDRATION PACK

Dehydration can be a bummer on a bike. It can not only make the ride home arduous, but it can be life-threatening on long, remote rides. A backpack with a hydration bladder in it allows you to carry a lot of water that can be accessed easily while riding. The bite valve on the end of the drinking tube can be kept in your mouth as you bounce over rough terrain. Hands-free drinking has big benefits over water bottles for mountain-bike riding.

The backpack also allows you to carry extra food, clothes and tools. If you do not have a hydration pack, at least bring water bottles, and carry extra food, tools and clothes tied to your bike, around your waist, or in a jersey pocket.

Emergency repairs

"Always carry a flagon of whiskey in case of a snake bite, and furthermore, always carry a small snake."

— W.C. FIELDS

FLAT TIRES

Flat tires can be prevented with the use of some tire sealants; "Slime" is one that works well. The stuff is a viscous liquid with chopped fibers in it that plug holes in the tube as they happen. It can be injected into your tube, or you can purchase tubes with sealant already inside.

If you have Slime or another tire sealant in your tube and your tire gets low (this is most likely to happen when you stop riding for a while), put more air in and spin the wheel or ride for a couple of miles to get the sealant to flow out to the hole. A large hole will not be filled, although amazingly big holes can be plugged enough to get you home if you locate where the sealant is squirting out through the tire. Rotate the wheel so that spot is at the bottom and wait. The sealant may pool up enough there to plug the hole. Add more air and continue.

We recommend against plastic tire liners that go between the tire and tube. They are so stiff that they decrease traction and cornering ability. They can also slip sideways and cut into the tube.

There is, however, a new generation of liners made from Kevlar. These liners are considerably lighter than their stiff plastic counterparts. They are pretty expensive, though. A pair of "Spin Skins" for mountain bike tires can run around $33.

FIXING A FLAT

If you have a spare or a patch kit, a simple flat is easy to deal with. The first flat you get on a ride is most easily fixed by installing your spare tube. Make sure you remove all thorns from the tire and feel around the inside of the tire for any other sharp objects. Check the rim to see that your flat wasn't caused by a protruding spoke or nipple, a metal shard from the rim, or the edge of a spoke hole protruding through a worn rim strip. Many rim strips are simply inadequate, being either too narrow or prone to cracking or tearing. Metal hunks left from the drilling of rims during manufacture can work their way out into the tube. Try to deal with these problems before leaving on a backcountry ride by shaking out any

metal fragments and using good rim strips or a couple of layers of fiberglass packing tape (with those lengthwise super-strong fibers inside) as rim strips. If the hole in the tube is on the rim side, tire sealant will not fill the hole, since the liquid will be thrown to the outside when the wheel turns.

After you run out of spare tubes, additional flats must be patched.

TORN SIDEWALL

Rocks and glass can cut tire sidewalls. The likelihood of this problem is reduced if you do not venture into the backcountry on old tires with rotten and weakened sidewall cords. If your tire's sidewall is torn or cut, the tube will stick out. Just patching or replacing the tube isn't going to solve the problem. Without reinforcement, your tube will blow out again very soon. First, you have to look for something to reinforce the sidewall. Dollar bills work surprisingly well as tire boots. The paper is

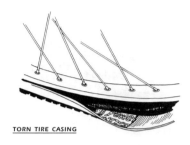

TORN TIRE CASING

vent it from bulging out through the hole in the side wall.

2. Put a little air in the tube to hold the makeshift reinforcement in place.

3. Mount the tire bead on the rim. You may need to let a little air out of the tube to do so.

4. After making sure that the tire is seated and the boot is still in place, inflate the tube to about 40 psi, if you are good at estimating without a gauge. Much less than 40 psi will allow the boot to move around and may also lead to a pinch flat if you're riding on rocky terrain. This is not a perfect solution, so you will need to check the boot periodically to make certain that the tube is not bulging out again.

pretty tough and should hold for the rest of the ride if you are careful. Business cards are a bit small, but work better than nothing (But then you gotta wonder why on earth you would bring your business cards on a ride!). You might even try an energy bar wrapper. A small piece of a tire liner cut in an oval might be a good addition to your patch kit for this purpose. You get the idea.

1. Lay the cash or whatever inside the tire over the gash, or wrap it around the tube at that spot. Place several layers between the tire and tube to support the tube and pre-

No more spare tubes or patches

Now comes the frustrating part: You have run out of spare tubes, and have used up all of your patches (or your CO_2 cartridge is empty and you don't have a pump), and still you have a flat tire. The solution is obvious. You are going to have to ride home without air in your tire. Riding a flat for a long way will trash your tire and will probably damage your rim. Still, there are ways to minimize that damage. Try filling the space in the tire with grass, leaves or similar materials. Pack it in tightly and then remount the tire on the rim. This should make the ride a little less dangerous, by minimizing the flat tire's tendency to roll out from under the bike during a turn.

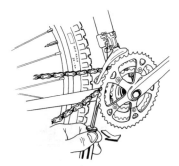

FREEING JAMMED CHAIN

CHAIN JAMMED BETWEEN THE CHAINRING AND CHAINSTAY

If your chain gets jammed between the chainrings and chainstay, it may be hard to get out if the clearance is tight. You may find that you tug and tug on the chain, and it won't come out. Well, chainrings flex, and if you apply some mechanical advantage, the chain will come free quite easily. Just insert a screwdriver or similar thin lever between the chainring and the chainstay, and pry the space open while pulling the chain out. You will probably be amazed at how easy this is, especially in light of how much hard tugging would not free the chain.

If you still cannot free the chain, disassemble the chain with a chain tool, pull it out, and put it back together.

BROKEN CHAIN

Chains break quite often while mountain-bike riding, usually while shifting the front derailleur under load. The side force of the derailleur on the chain coupled with the high tension can pop a chain plate off the end of a rivet. As the chain rips apart, it can cause collateral damage as well. The open chain plate can snag the front derailleur cage, bending it or tearing it off, or it can jam into the rear dropout.

When a chain breaks, the end link is certainly shot, and some others in the area may be as well.

1. Remove the damaged links with the chain tool. (You did remember to bring a chain tool, right?)

2. If you have brought along extra chain links, replace the same number you remove. If not, you'll need to use the chain in its shortened state; it will still work.

3. Join the ends and connect the chain (Illustration). Some light-weight chain tools and multi tools are more difficult to use than a

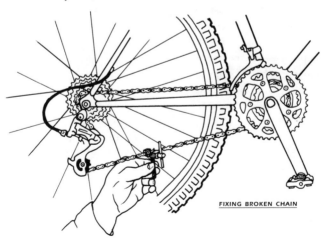

FIXING BROKEN CHAIN

FIXING A BENT RIM

shop chain tool. Some flex so badly that it is hard to keep the push rod lined up with the rivet. Others pinch the plates so tightly that the chain link binds up. It's a good idea to find these things out before you attempt repairs on the trail. Try the tool out at home or at your local bike shop. This way you know what you're getting into before you reach the trailhead.

BENT WHEEL

If the rim is banging against the brake pads, or worse yet the frame or fork, pedaling becomes very difficult. It can happen due to either a loose or broken spoke, or due to a badly bent or broken rim.

BENT RIM

If your rim is only mildly out of true, and you brought your spoke wrench, you can fix it.

If the wheel is really whacked out, spoke truing won't do much to get it to clear the brakes so that you can pedal home.

If the wheel is bent to the point that it won't turn, even when the brake is removed, you can beat it straight as long as the rim is not broken.

1. Find the area that is bent outward the most and mark it.
2. Leaving the tire on and inflated, hold the wheel by its sides with the bent part at the top facing away from you.
3. Smack the bent section of the rim against the flat ground
4. Put the wheel back in the frame or fork, and see if anything has changed.
5. Repeat the process until the wheel is rideable. You may be

surprised how straight you can get a wheel this way.

LOOSE SPOKES

If you have a loose spoke or two, the rim will wobble all over the place.
1. Find the loose spoke (or spokes) by feeling all of them. The really loose ones, which would cause a wobble of large magnitude, will be obvious. If you find a broken spoke, skip to the next section. If you have no loose or broken spokes, skip.
2. Get out the spoke wrench that you carry for such an eventuality. If you don't have one, skip to the section below.
3. Mark the loose spokes by tying blades of grass, sandwich bag twist-ties, tape or the like around them.
4. Tighten the loose spokes, and true the wheel.

BROKEN SPOKES

If you broke a spoke, the wheel will wobble wildly.
1. Locate the broken spoke.

LOOSE SPOKE

2. Remove the remainder of the spoke, both the piece going through the hub, and the piece threaded into the nipple. If the broken spoke is on the freewheel side of the rear wheel, you may not be able to remove it from the hub, since it will be behind the cogs. If so, skip to step 6 after wrapping it around neighboring spokes to prevent it from slapping around.
3. Get out your spoke wrench.
4. If you brought a spare spoke of the right length or one of those nifty Kevlar replacement spokes we mentioned at the beginning of this manual, you're in business.

Put the new spoke through the hub hole, weave it through the other spokes the same way the old one

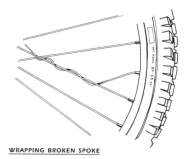

WRAPPING BROKEN SPOKE

was, and thread it into the spoke nipple that is still sticking out of the rim. Mark it with a pen or a blade of grass tied around it. With the Kevlar spoke, thread the Kevlar through the hub hole, attach the ends to the enclosed stub of spoke, adjust the ends to length, tie them off, and tighten the spoke nipple.

5. Tighten the nipple on the new spoke with a spoke wrench, checking the rim clearance with the brake pad as you go. Stop when the rim is straight, and finish your ride.

6. If you can't replace the spoke but you do have a spoke wrench, bring the wheel into rideable trueness by loosening the spoke on either side of the broken one. These two spokes come from the opposite side of the hub and will let the rim move toward the side with the broken spoke as they are loosened. A spoke nipple loosens clockwise when viewed from its top. Ride home, conservatively, as this wheel will rapidly get worse.

7. Once at home, replace the spoke or take the wheel to a bike shop for repair. After you have had a broken spoke more than once on a wheel, it should be re-laced with new spokes, and the rim may need replacement as well.

BROKEN FRONT DERAILLEUR CABLE

Your chain will be on the inner chainring, and you will still be able to use all of your rear cogs. You have three options, depending on which chainring you want for your return ride:

OPTION 1 Leave it on the inner

ring and ride home.

OPTION 2 Tighten the inner derailleur stop screw until the derailleur sits over the middle chainring. Leave the chain on the middle ring and ride home.

OPTION 3 Bypass the front derailleur by removing the chain from the derailleur and putting it on the big chainring. You can do this either by opening the derailleur cage with a screwdriver or by disconnecting and reconnecting the chain with a chain tool.

Note: You have probably noticed by now that a chain tool is one of the handiest items you can take along. Like the American Express ads say: "Don't leave home without it."

BROKEN REAR DERAILLEUR CABLE

Your chain will be on the smallest rear cog, and you will still be able to use all three front chainrings. You have three options:

OPTION 1 Leave it as is and ride home.

OPTION 2 Move the chain to a larger cog, push inward on the derailleur with your hand, and tighten the high-end adjustment screw on the rear derailleur (usually the upper one of the two screws) until it lines up with a larger cog. Move the chain to that cog and ride home. You may have to fine-tune the adjustment of the derailleur stop screw to get it to run quietly without skipping.

OPTION 3 If you do not have a screwdriver, you can push inward on the rear derailleur while turning the crank with the rear wheel off of the ground to shift to a larger cog. Jam a stick in between the derailleur cage plates to prevent it from moving back down to the small cog.

BROKEN BRAKE CABLE

Ride home very slowly and very carefully if the trail is not dangerous. If it is dangerous, walk.

The drive train

"(I) express my joy, for now no more do I cower in terror of the chain."

"BACCHANTES," EURIPIDES, 406 B.C.

You have a new bike. It fits and your legs are strong. Now go out and enjoy … just remember that it takes an elaborate system of pulleys, cables, derailleurs and a chain to transfer all that power in your legs into forward motion. The drivetrain is the real heart of a bicycle and to run efficiently it has to be regularly cleaned and maintained. The good news is that the proper care and feeding of that drivetrain involves a pretty simple set of steps.

THE CHAIN

A bike chain is a not-so-simple series of links connected by rivets. Rollers surround each rivet between the link plates and engage the teeth of the cogs and chainrings. It is an extremely efficient method of transmitting mechanical energy from your pedals to your rear wheel. In terms of weight, cost and efficiency, the bicycle chain has no equal … lots and lots of people have tried to improve on it.

To keep your bike running smoothly, you do have to pay at least some attention to your chain. It needs to be kept clean and well-lubricated in order to utilize your energy most efficiently, shift smoothly, and maximize chain life. Chains need to be replaced regularly to prolong the working life of other, more expensive, components. This is because, as a chain's internal parts wear, it gets longer, thus contacting gear teeth differently than intended.

LUBRICATION

Lubricate your chain regularly — after every ride in wet conditions, a little less often in a dry environment. When lubricating the chain, use a lubricant intended for bicycle chains. If you want to get fancy about it, you can even pick one specifically designed for the conditions in which you ride.

1. Drip a small amount of lubricant across each roller, periodically moving the chain to give easy access to the links you are working on. If you are in a hurry, you can turn the crank slowly while dripping lubricant onto the chain as it goes by. This is better than not lubricating the chain, but it will cause you to apply too much lubricant. That, in turn, will cause the chain to pick up dirt faster, and you will wear out your chain sooner.

2. Wipe the chain off lightly with a rag.

KEEP IT CLEAN

Cleaning the chain can be accomplished in a number of ways.

The simplest way to maintain a chain is to wipe it down frequently and then lubricate it. If this is done prior to every ride, you will never need to clean your chain with a solvent. The lubricant softens the old sludge buildup, which is driven out of the chain when you ride. The problem is that the lubricant also picks up new dirt and grime.

If you use one of the new chain waxes (wax mixed with solvent) and you apply it frequently, the chain will stay very clean as well as lubricated. Chain cleaning can be performed with the bike standing on the ground or in a bike stand.

LUBING CHAIN

1. With a rag in your hand, grasp the lower length of the chain (between the bottom of the chainring and the rear derailleur lower jockey wheel).

2. Turn the crank backward a number of revolutions, pulling the chain through the rag. Periodically rotate the rag to present a cleaner section of it to the chain.

3. Lubricate each chain roller as above.

CHAIN-CLEANING UNITS

Several companies make chain-cleaning units that scrub the chain with solvent while it is still on the bike. These types of chain cleaners are generally made of clear plastic and have two or three rotating brushes that scrub the chain as it moves through the solvent bath. These units offer the advantage of letting you clean your chain without removing it from the bike.

REMOVAL AND CLEANING

You can also clean the chain by removing it from the bicycle and cleaning it in a solvent. We recommend against it, because repeated disassembly weakens the chain, unless you use a chain with a master link.

Chain disassembly and reassembly expands the size of the rivet hole where you put it together, allowing the rivet to pop out more easily. Shimano supplies special "subpins" for reassembly of their chains that are meant to prevent this. A hand-opened "master link" can avoid the chain weakening of pushing pins out. Master links are standard on Taya chains and will be on Sachs chains of 1998 and beyond; the aftermarket "Super Link" from Lickton Cycle can also be installed into any chain.

If you do disassemble the chain, you can clean it well, even without a solvent tank. Just drop your chain into an old jar or water bottle half filled with solvent. Using an old water bottle or jar allows you to clean the chain without touching or breathing the solvent — something to be avoided even with citrus solvents.

When you're finished, hang the chain to air dry, reinstall it and don't forget to lubricate it before you ride.

CHAIN REPLACEMENT

As the rollers, pins and plates wear out, your chain will begin to get longer. That, in turn, will hasten the wear and tear on the other parts of your drivetrain. An elongated chain will concentrate the load on each individual gear tooth, rather than distributing it over all of the teeth that the chain contacts. This will result in the gear teeth becoming hook-shaped and the tooth valleys becoming wider. If such wear has already occurred, a new chain will not solve the problem. A new chain will not mesh with deformed teeth, and it is likely to skip whenever you pedal hard. So, before all of that extra wear and tear takes place, get in the habit of replacing your chain on a regular basis.

How long it takes for the chain to "stretch" will vary, depending on chain type, maintenance, riding conditions, and strength and weight of the rider. Figure on replacing your chain every 500 to 1000 miles, especially if ridden in dirty conditions by a large rider. Lighter riders riding mostly on paved roads can extend replacement time to 2000 miles.

CHECKING FOR CHAIN ELONGATION

The simplest method is to employ a chain-elongation indicator, such as the model made by Rohloff. The indicator falls completely into the chain if the chain is too worn. If the chain is still in good shape, the indicator's tooth will not go all of the way in.

Another way is to measure it with an accurate ruler. Chains are measured on an inch standard, and there should be exactly an integral num-

CHECKING CHAIN ELONGATION

ONE COMPLETE CHAIN LINK

ber of links in one foot.

1. Set one end of the ruler on a rivet edge, and measure to the rivet edge at the other end of the ruler.

2. The distance between these rivets should be exactly 12 inches. If it is 12 1/8 inches or greater — even 12 1/16 inches — go ahead and replace it. Chain manufacturer Sachs recommends replacement if elongation is 1 percent, or 1/2-inch in 100 links. If the chain is off of the bike, you can hang it next to a new chain; if it is more than a half-link longer for the same number of links, replace it.

CHAIN REMOVAL

1. Place any link over the back teeth on a chain tool.

2. Tighten the chain-tool handle clockwise to push the link rivet out. Unless you have a Shimano

chain and a new "subpin" for it (in which case you push the rivet completely out), be careful to leave a millimeter or so of rivet protruding inward from the chain plate to hook the chain back together when reassembling.

CHAIN INSTALLATION

1. Determine the chain length:

METHOD 1 Assuming your old chain was the correct length, compare the two and use the same number of links.

METHOD 2 If you have a standard long-cage mountain bike rear derailleur on your bike, wrap the chain around the big chainring and the biggest cog without going through either derailleur. Bring the two ends together until the ends

REMOVING RIVET

overlap; one full link should be the amount of overlap. Remove the remaining links, and save them in your spare tire bag so you have spares in case of chain breakage on the trail.

2. Route the chain properly:

Shift the derailleurs so that the chain will rest on the smallest cog in the rear and on the smallest chainring up front.

Starting with the rear derailleur pulley that is farthest from the derailleur body (this will be the bottom pulley once the chain is taut), guide the chain up through the rear derailleur, going around the two jockey pulleys. Make sure the chain passes inside of the prongs on the rear derailleur cage.

• Guide the chain over the smallest rear cog.

• Guide the chain through the front derailleur cage.

• Wrap the chain around the smallest front chainring.

• Bring the chain ends together so they meet.

3. Connect the chain:

Connecting a chain is much easier if the link rivet that was partially removed when the chain was taken apart is facing toward you. Positioning the link rivet this way allows you to use the chain tool in a much more comfortable manner (driving the rivet toward the bike, instead of back at you).

CABLES AND HOUSINGS

In order for the derailleurs to function properly, you need to have clean, smooth-running cables. Because of all the muck and guck that you encounter on a mountain bike, you need to regularly replace those cables. As with replacing a chain, replacing cables is a maintenance operation, not a repair operation. Do not wait until cables break to replace them. Replace any cables that have broken strands, kinks or fraying between the shifter and the derailleur. You should also replace the outer housing if any part of it is bent, mashed, just plain gritty or the color clashes with your bike (this last point is, of course, critical!).

PREPARING CABLE AND HOUSING FOR REPLACEMENT

1. Buy new cables and housing with at least as much length as the ones you are replacing.

2. Make sure that the cables and housing are for indexed systems. These cables will stretch minimally, and the housings will not compress in length. Under its external plastic sheath, indexed housing is not made of steel coil like brake housings; it is made of parallel (coaxial) steel strands of thin wire. If you look at the end, you will see numerous wire ends sticking out surrounding a central Teflon tube (make sure it has this Teflon liner, too).

3. Buy a few cable crimp caps to prevent fraying, and a tubular cable housing end (ferrule) for each end of every housing section. These ferrules will prevent kinking at the cable entry points, cable stops, shifters and derailleurs.

While you're at it, buying rubber cable donuts or sheathing for barecable runs is worthwhile to protect your frame.

4. Cut the housing to the same lengths as your old ones. Use a special cable cutter because standard wire cutters will not cut index-shift housing.

5. With a nail or toothpick, open each Teflon sleeve-end that has been smashed shut by the cutter.

6. Place a ferrule over each housing end.

REPLACING CABLE

THUMBSHIFTERS AND EARLY RAPID-FIRE

CABLE TYPES AND HOUSINGS

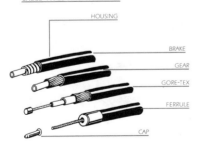

HOUSING

BRAKE

GEAR

GORE-TEX

FERRULE

CAP

1. Shift both levers to the gear setting that lets the most cable out. This will be the highest gear position for the rear shift lever (small cog), and the lowest for the front (small ring).

2. Pull out the old cable and recycle it.

3. The recessed hole into which the cable head seats should be visible right up against the barrel adjuster. Thread the cable through the hole and out through the barrel adjuster.

4. Guide the cable through each housing segment and cable stop. Slotted cable stops on the frame allow you to slip the cable and housing in and out from the side.

XTR RAPID-FIRE

Shimano XTR shifters sold in 1996 and later have a plastic cover over the wire-end hook and also have a slotted barrel adjuster and shifter body.

1. Shift the smaller (upper and forward) finger-operated lever until the shifter lets out all of the cable.

2. Turn the shifter barrel-adjuster so the cable slit is lined up with the slot in the shifter body; the slot is on the opposite side from the gear indicator.

3. Unscrew the Phillips-head screw on the plastic cover; it will not come completely out (where you could lose it), being retained in the cover by a plastic ring. Open the cover.

4. Pull the old cable down out of the slot, and pull the cable head out of the hook.

5. Slip the new cable head into the

THUMB SHIFTER

RAPIDFIRE SHIFTER

cable hook, and pull the cable into the slot. Turn the barrel adjuster so the slots no longer line up.

6. Close the cover and tighten the screw (gently!).

7. Guide the cable through each housing segment and cable stop. Slotted cable stops allow you to slip the cable and housing in and out from the side.

Note: Replacing the thin cables connected to the XTR "Rapid-fire Remote" bar-end-mounted shifters requires buying the thin double-headed cables and housings from Shimano. The small heads simply slip through the holes in both sets of shift levers (on the bar and on the bar end) from the back side. You install the little plastic cable head caps onto the metal cable heads to keep them from pulling back through. That's it!

GRIP SHIFT

The Grip Shift lever must be disassembled to replace the cable.

1. Disconnect the derailleur cable.

2. Roll or slide the handlebar grip away from the Grip Shift to allow room for the shifter to slide apart.

3. With a Phillips screwdriver, remove the triangular plastic cover holding the two main sections together.

4. Pull the outer shifter section away from the main body to separate it from the inner housing. Watch for the spring to ensure that it does not fall out. It can be nudged back into place if it does.

5. Pull the old cable out and recycle it.

6. Clean and dry the two parts if they are dirty; a rag and a cotton swab are usually sufficient. Finish Line offers a cleaning and grease kit specifically designed for Grip Shift shifters. A really gummed-up shifter may require solvent and compressed air to clean and dry it.

7. Using a non-lithium grease, lubricate the inner housing tube and spring cavity, all cable grooves, and the indexing notches in the

twister. Grip Shift recommends a silicone-based Teflon grease; SRAM and Finish Line sell such lubes.

8. Thread the cable through the hole, seating the cable end in its little pocket.

9. For the rear shifter, loop the cable once around the housing tube, and exit it through the barrel adjuster. For the front shifter, the cable routes directly into its guide.

10. Make sure the spring is in its cavity in the housing; hold the spring in with a small amount of grease if need be.

ATTACHING REAR DERAILLEUR CABLE

11. Slide the outer (twister) body over the inner tube. Be sure that the shifter is in the position that lets the most cable out. (On models with numbers, line up the highest number with the indicator mark on rear shifters, lowest number on front shifters.)

12. Lift the cable loop into the groove in the twister, and push straight inward on it as you pull tension on the cable exiting the shifter. The twister should slide in until flush under the housing edge; you may have to jiggle it back and forth slightly while push-ing in to get it properly seated.

13. Replace the cover and screw.

14. Check that the shifter clicks properly.

15. Slide the grip back into place.

16. Guide the cable through each housing segment and cable stop. Slotted cable stops allow you to slip the cable and housing in and out from the side.

ATTACHING CABLE TO THE REAR DERAILLEUR

1. Put the chain on the smallest

cog so the rear derailleur moves to the outside.

2. Run the cable through the barrel adjuster, and route it through each of the housing segments until you reach the cable-fixing bolt on the derailleur. Make sure that the rear shifter is on the highest setting; this ensures that the maximum amount of cable is available to the derailleur.

3. Pull the cable taut and into its groove under the cable-fixing bolt.

4. Tighten the bolt. On most derailleurs

PULL CABLE TIGHT BEFORE TIGHTENING WITH ALLEN WRENCH

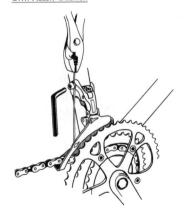

this takes a 5mm Allen wrench.

<u>ATTACHING CABLE TO THE FRONT DERAILLEUR</u>

1. Operate the shifter to allow the most cable out (granny gear setting). Shift the chain to the inner ring so that the derailleur moves farthest to the inside.

2. Connect the cable to the cable-anchor groove under the bolt on the derailleur arm while pulling the cable taut with pliers. Make sure you do not hook up a top-pull front derailleur from the bottom, or vice versa. Some older derailleur models require housing to run all of the way to a stop on the derailleur.

TWEAKS AND ADJUSTMENTS

<u>ADJUSTMENT OF REAR DERAILLEUR AND RIGHT-HAND SHIFTER</u>

Perform all of the following derailleur adjustments with the bike in a bike stand or hung from the ceiling. That way, you can turn the

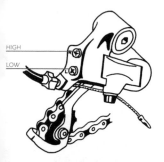

HIGH

LOW

LIMIT SCREWS AND BARREL ADJUSTER

crank and shift gears while you put
the derailleur through its paces.
After adjustment off of the ground,
test the shifting while riding.
Derailleurs often perform differently under load than in a bike stand.

LIMIT SCREW ADJUSTMENTS

The first, and most important, rear
derailleur adjustment is the limit
screws. Properly set, these screws
should make certain that you will
not ruin your frame, wheel or
derailleur by shifting into the spokes
or by jamming the chain between the
dropout and the smallest cog. It is
never pleasant to see your expensive

equipment turned into shredded
metal. All it takes is a small screwdriver to turn these limit screws.
Remember, it's lefty loosey, righty
tighty for these screws.

HIGH-GEAR-LIMIT SCREW ADJUSTMENT

This screw limits the outward
movement of the rear derailleur.
You tighten or loosen this screw
until the derailleur shifts the chain
to the smallest cog quickly but does
not overshift.

How do you determine which
limit screw works on the high gear?
Often, it will be labeled with an
"H," and it is usually the upper of
the two screws. If you're not certain,
try both screws. Whichever screw,
when tightened, moves the
derailleur inward when the chain is
on the smallest cog is the one you
are looking for. On most derailleurs,
you can also see which screw to
adjust by looking in between the
derailleur's parallelogram side
plates. You will see one tab on the
back end of each plate. Each is

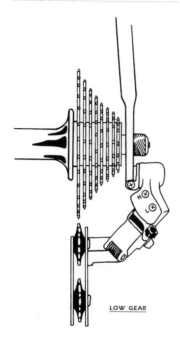

LOW GEAR

2. While slowly turning the crank, shift the rear derailleur to the smallest rear cog (highest gear).
3. If there is hesitation in the chain's shifting movement, loosen the cable a little to see if it is stopping the derailleur from moving out far enough (this does not apply to Rapid-Rise rear derailleurs). Do this by turning the barrel adjuster on the derailleur or shift lever clockwise, or by loosening the cable-fixing bolt.
4. If the chain still won't drop smoothly and without hesitation to the smallest cog, loosen the high-gear-limit screw a quarter turn at a time, continuously repeating the shift, until the chain repeatedly drops quickly and easily.
5. If the derailleur throws the chain into the dropout, or it tries to go past the smallest cog, tighten the high-gear-limit screw a quarter turn and re-do the shift. Repeat until the derailleur shifts the chain quickly and easily into the highest gear without throwing the chain into the dropout.

designed to hit a limit screw at one end of the movement. Shift into your highest gear, and notice which screw is touching one of the tabs; that is the high-gear-limit screw.
1. Shift the chain to the large front chain ring.

LOW-GEAR-LIMIT SCREW ADJUSTMENT

This screw stops the inward movement of the rear derailleur, preventing it from going into the spokes. This screw is usually labeled "L," and it is usually the bottom screw. You can check which one it is by shifting to the largest cog, maintaining pressure on the shifter, and turning the screw to see if it changes the position of the derailleur.

1. Shift the chain to the inner chain-ring on the front. Shift the rear derailleur to the lowest gear (largest cog). Do it gently, in case the limit screw does not stop the derailleur from going into the spokes.

2. If the derailleur touches the spokes or shoves the chain over the largest cog, tighten the low-gear-limit screw until it does not.

3. If the derailleur cannot bring the chain onto the largest cog, loosen the screw a quarter turn. Repeat this step until the chain shifts easily up to the cog, but does not touch the spokes.

Final details of rear derailleur adjustment:

"B-SCREW" ADJUSTMENT

You can get a bit more precision by adjusting the small screw ("B-screw") that changes the derailleur's position against the derailleur hanger tab on the right rear dropout. Viewing from behind with the chain on the inner chainring and largest cog, adjust the screw so that the upper jockey wheel is close to the cog, but not pinching the chain against the cog. Repeat on the smallest cog. You'll know that you've moved it in too closely when it starts making noise.

SRAM (a.k.a.: Grip Shift) suggests setting the B-screw on its ESP derailleurs with the chain on the middle chainring and largest cog.

SHIFTER MAINTENANCE
GRIP SHIFT

Grip Shift shifters require periodic lubrication. The exploded diagrams

GRIP SHIFT RIGHT SHIFTER

GRIP SHIFT LEFT SHIFTER

detail how to take a shifter apart, clean it and grease it. Use only non-lithium (preferably silicone-based Teflon) grease. As long as you have the shifter disassembled, you might as well replace the cable.

RAPID-FIRE SL AND RAPID-FIRE PLUS

Shimano Rapid-fire SL and Rapid-fire Plus shifters are not designed to be disassembled by the consumer. Squirting a little chain lube inside every now and then is a good idea, though. If a Rapid-fire Plus lever stops working, it requires purchasing a new shifter unit. The brake lever does not need to be replaced; just bolt the new shifter to it.

Sometimes the gear indicator unit stops working, and it can even jam the lever and stop it from

reaching all of the gears. This was most common in the 1993 and 1994 models. The indicators can be removed from the shifter with a small screwdriver. The indicator's link arm needs to be stuck back into the hole from whence it came. Once the indicator jams, you can expect it to happen again; eventually, you will want to replace the lever or you could just dispense with the indicator.

THUMB SHIFTERS

Indexed (click) thumb shifters are also not to be disassembled beyond simply removing them from their clamp. Periodic (semi-annual or so) lubrication with chain lube is recommended and is best accomplished from the back side once the shifter assembly is removed from its clamp.

Frictional (non-clicking) thumb shifters can be disassembled, cleaned, greased, and reassembled. Put the parts back the way you found them. You can avoid the hassle of disassembly by squirting chain lube in instead.

CHAINRINGS AND CRANK

You should get into the habit of checking your chainrings regularly. They do wear out and need to be replaced. It's hard to say how often, so include chainrings as part of your regular maintenance checklist. Check your chainrings for wear, when you replace your chain.

Check your crankarms periodically for cracks and tightness.

Inspect the crankarms for cracks all over, but particularly in three areas where they are most likely to develop. Check around the hole at the top of each arm that slips onto

the bottom bracket spindle. On the right crank, check in the crotch between each pair of spider arms (the struts that bolt to the chainrings), and especially in each crotch between each of the lower two spider arms and the crankarm. Finally, check around each pedal-spindle hole.

Make sure the crank bolt holding each crankarm to the bottom bracket spindle is tight. If you have a torque wrench, tighten each bolt to the torque specification in the torque table in the back of this book. If not, tighten the bolts tightly with a socket wrench (usually 14mm). The torque specification is very tight on these, so tighten it down well. Make sure you do not have a titanium crank bolt tightening into a titanium spindle, as the two parts will gall and bind. If you have a titanium crank bolt (with a steel bottom bracket spindle), replace it with a steel one for purposes of tightening the crank on to the specified torque, then remove the steel bolt and tighten the titanium one in. The titanium bolt will stretch and will not tighten the crank on as far by itself as a steel one can.

BOTTOM BRACKET

Your bottom bracket should spin smoothly and freely without side-to-side play in the spindle.

Check for freedom of motion after flipping the chain off to the inside so that it does not drag on the chainrings. Spin the crank. It should spin easily and continue spinning for some time. It should not stop suddenly; rather, it should swing back and forth around its stopping point as it runs out of momentum. Some bottom brackets are sealed so well against contamination that it restricts their freedom of rotation. If your crank does not spin very long before stopping, but it turns

smoothly with no binding or gritty, crunching feel or sound, then it is probably well-sealed and in good shape.

If you hear or feel grit and/or crunching in the bottom bracket, it needs to be overhauled or replaced.

If the bottom bracket does not spin freely and rolls roughly, but it does not feel gritty, then it may simply be adjusted too tightly. Adjustment is covered in chapter eight of "Zinn and the Art of Mountain Bike Maintenance," or you can have it done by a bike shop.

Check that your bottom bracket is not adjusted too loosely as well. With your crankarms lined up with the seat tube or the down tube, push the top arm back and forth toward the frame and see if it clunks back and forth. You should feel no play, flex or clunking. If the arm moves laterally back and forth relative to the frame, your bottom bracket is too loose.

CHAPTER 6
Wheels and tires

The wheel in fact was badly damaged. The collision with the mail wagon had broken two spokes and loosened the hub so that the nut no longer held. "My friend," said he to the stable-boy, "is there a wheelwright here?"

— *"Les Miserables," Victor Hugo, 1862*

Well, the wheelwright business ain't what it used to be, but for those of us who love to ride bikes, the neighborhood bike shop will usually do. Still, it's important to learn at least a few of the basics so that, in a pinch, you can change a tire or repair your wheels without having to run down to the local mechanic. This is especially true when you're on the road or tooling around out in the boonies.

The critical first step in all of this is simply learning the right way to remove and replace your wheel.

WHEEL REMOVAL
RELEASING THE BRAKE

Most brakes have a mechanism to release the brake arms so that they spring away from the rim, allowing the tire to pass between the pads. V-brakes are released by pulling the end of the curved cable guide tube (a.k.a. the "noodle") out of the horizontal link atop one of the brake arms while squeezing the pads against the rim with the other hand. Most cantilevers and U-brakes are released by pulling the enlarged head of the straddle cable out of a notch in the top of the brake arm while holding the pads against the rim with the other hand.

Roller-cam brakes are released by pulling the cam down and out from between the two rollers while holding the pads against the rim. Many linkage brakes are released like V-brakes or cantilevers. Hydraulic rim brakes usually require detaching the U-shaped brake booster that connects the piston cylinders together, if installed, followed by unscrewing or quick-releasing one wheel cylinder. Most disc brakes allow the disc to fall away without releasing the pads. The Dia Compe disc brake requires opening a latch under the caliper securing it to the fork. The entire caliper can then be swung up and forward, allowing the wheel to come out.

<u>UNDOING THE QUICK-RELEASE SKEWER</u>

This is so easy that you don't even need a tool for this one.

TIGHTENING THE QUICK RELEASE

1. Pull the lever out to open it.

2. After opening the quick-release lever, unscrew the nut on the opposite end of the quick-release skewer's shaft until it clears the fork's wheel retention tabs.

3. Pull the wheel off.

Note: Some bikes have non-quick-release superlight titanium bolt-on skewers. The wheel is removed by unscrewing the skewer with a 5mm Allen wrench.

<u>REPLACING A WHEEL WITH A QUICK-RELEASE SKEWER</u>

The quick-release skewer is not a glorified wing nut and should not be treated as such.

1. Hold the quick release-lever in the "open" position.

2. Tighten the opposite end nut until it snugs up against the face of the dropout.

3. Push the lever over to the "closed" position (it should now be at a 90-degree angle to the axle). It should take a good amount of hand pressure to close the quick-release

lever properly; the lever should leave its imprint on your palm for a few seconds.

4. If the quick-release lever does not close tightly, open the lever again, tighten the end nut 1/4 turn and close the lever again. Repeat until tight.

5. If, on the other hand, the lever cannot be pushed down perpendicular to the axle, then the nut is too tight. Open the quick-release lever, unscrew the end nut 1/4 turn or so, and try closing the lever again. Repeat this procedure until the quick-release lever is fully closed and snug.

When you are done, it is important to have the lever pointing straight up or toward the back of the bike so that it cannot hook on obstacles and be accidentally opened.

6. Check that the axle is tightened into the fork by trying to pull the wheel out.

7. Reconnect the brakes and you're done!

SCHRADER VALVE

TIRES AND TUBES

REPLACING OR REPAIRING TIRES AND INNER TUBES

1. Remove the wheel like we just told you to.

2. If your tire is not already flat, deflate it.

To deflate a Schrader valve (the kind of valve you would find on your car's tire), push down on the valve pin with something thin enough to fit in that won't break off, like a pen cap or a paper clip.

Presta, or "French," valves are thinner and have a small threaded rod with a tiny nut on the end. To let air out, unscrew the little nut a few turns, and push down on the thin rod. To seal, tighten the little nut down again (with your fingers only!); leave it tightened down for riding.

Note: If you have deep-section rims (like Spinergy, Zipp or Hed), you will probably have valve extenders — thin threaded tubes that screw onto the valve.

3. If you can push the tire bead off of the rim with your thumbs without using tire levers, by all means do it, since there is less chance of damaging either the tube or the tire.

4. If you can't get it off with your hands alone, insert a tire lever, scoop side up, between the rim sidewall and the tire until you catch the edge of the tire bead.

5. Push down on the lever until the tire bead is pulled out over the rim. If the lever has a hook on the other end, hook it onto the nearest spoke. Otherwise, keep holding it down.

6. Place the next lever a few inches away, and do the same thing with it.

7. If needed, place a third lever a few inches farther on, pry it out, and continue sliding this lever around the tire, pulling the bead out as you go. Some people use their fingers under the bead to slide the tire off, but beware of cutting your fingers on sharp tire beads.

8. Once the bead is off on one side,

REMOVING TIRES WITH LEVERS

INSTALLING TIRE BY HAND

pull the tube out. If you are patching or replacing the tube, you do not need to remove the other side of the tire from the rim. If you are replacing the tire, the other bead should come off easily with your fingers. If it does not, use the tire levers.

INSTALLING PATCHED OR NEW TUBE

Feel around the inside of the tire to see if there is still anything sticking through that can puncture the tube. This is best done by sliding a rag all the way around the inside of the tire. The rag will catch on anything sharp, and saves your fingers from being cut by whatever is stuck in the tire.

1. Replace any tire that has worn-out areas (inside or out) where the tread-casing fibers appear to be cut or frayed.

2. Examine the rim to be certain that the rim tape is in place and that there are no spokes or anything else sticking up that can puncture the tube. Replace the rim tape if necessary.

3. By hand, push one side bead of the tire onto the rim.

4. (Optional) Smear talcum powder around the inside of the tire and on the outside of the tube, so the two

do not adhere to each other.

5. Put just enough air in the tube to give it shape. Close the valve, if Presta.

6. Push the valve through the valve hole in the rim.

7. Push the tube up inside the tire all of the way around.

8. Starting at the side opposite the valve stem, push the tire bead onto the rim with your thumbs. Be sure that the tube doesn't get pinched between the tire bead and the rim.

9. Work around the rim in both directions with your thumbs, pushing the tire onto the rim. Finish from both sides at the valve. You can usually install a mountain bike tire without tools. If you cannot, use tire levers, but make sure you don't catch any of the tube under the edge of the bead. Finish the same way, at the valve.

10. Re-seat the valve stem by pushing up on the valve after you have pushed the last bit of bead onto the rim. You may have to manipulate the tire so that all the tube is tucked under the tire bead.

11. Go around the rim and inspect for any part of the tube that might be protruding out from under the edge of the tire bead. If you have a fold of the tube under the edge of the bead, it can blow the tire off the rim either when you inflate it or while you are riding. It will sound like a gun went off next to you and will leave you with an unpatchable tube.

12. Pump up the tire. Generally, 45-50 psi is a good amount. Much more, and the ride gets harsh. Much less, and you run the risk of a pinch flat or "snake bite."

PATCHING AN INNER TUBE

1. If the leak location is not obvious, put some air in the tube to inflate it until it is two to three times larger than its deflated size. Be careful. You can explode it if you put too much air in, especially with latex or urethane tubes.

2. Listen/feel for air coming out, and mark the leak(s).

3. If you cannot find the leak by lis-

tening, submerge the tube under water. Look for air bubbling out, and mark the spot(s).

Keep in mind that you can only patch small holes. If the hole is bigger than the eraser end of a pencil, a round patch is not likely to work. A slit of up to an inch or so can be repaired with a long, oval patch.

STANDARD PATCHES

1. Dry the tube thoroughly near the hole.
2. Rough up and clean the surface about a 1-inch radius around the hole with a small piece of sandpaper (usually supplied with the patch kit). Do not touch the sanded area, and don't rough up the tube with one of those little metal "cheese graters" that come with some patch kits. (They tend to do to your tube what they do to cheese.)
3. Use a patch kit designed for bicycle tires that have the thin, usually orange, gummy edges surrounding the black patches. Rema and Delta are common brands.
4. Apply patch cement in a thin,

smooth layer all over an area centered on the hole. Cover an area that is bigger than the size of the patch.
5. Let the glue dry until there are no more shiny, wet spots.
6. Remove the foil backing from the patch (but not the cellophane top cover).
7. Stick the patch over the hole, and push it down in place, making sure that all of the gummy edges are stuck down.
8. Remove the cellophane top covering, being careful not to peel off the edges of the patch. Often, the cellophane top patch is scored. If you fold the patch, this cellophane will split at the scored cuts, allowing you to peel outward and avoid pulling the newly-adhered patch away from the tube.

GLUELESS PATCHES

There are a number of adhesive-backed patches on the market that do not require cement to stick them on. Most often, you simply need to clean the area around the hole with the little alcohol pad supplied with the patch. Let the alcohol dry, peel the backing, and stick on the patch. The advantage of glueless patches is that they are very fast to use, take little room in a seat bag, and you never open your patch kit to discover that your glue tube is dried up. On the downside, I have not found any that stick nearly as well as the standard type. With a standard patch installed, you can inflate the tube to look for more leaks without having to put the tube back in the tire. If you do that with a glueless patch, it usually lifts the patch enough to start it leaking. You must install it in the tire and on the rim before putting air in it after patching.

PATCHING TIRE CASING (SIDE WALL)

Unless it is an emergency, don't do it! If your casing is cut, get a new tire. Patching the tire casing is dangerous. No matter what you use as a patch, the tube will find a way to bulge out of the patched hole, and when it does your tire will go flat immediately. In emergency situations, follow the instructions we outlined in Chapter 2. Then, when you get home, replace the tire ASAP!

RIMS & SPOKES
TRUING A WHEEL

This is not meant as a guide for building wheels. If you want to know that you should probably go out and buy a book. Indeed, even though we wrote it, we still like to recommend Velo Press's "Zinn and the Art of Mountain-bike Maintenance" as a reasonably good guide to the mysteries of wheel construction. For now, we'll just try to deal with loose spokes, dinged wheels and miscellaneous wiggles and wobbles.

If your wheel has a wobble in it, you can fix it by adjusting the tension on the spokes. An extreme bend in the rim cannot be fixed by spoke truing alone, since the spoke tension on the two sides of the wheel will be so uneven that the

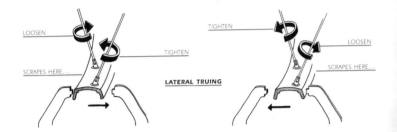

LOOSEN
TIGHTEN
SCRAPES HERE...

TIGHTEN
LOOSEN
SCRAPES HERE...

LATERAL TRUING

wheel will rapidly fall apart.

1. Check that there are no broken spokes in the wheel, or any spokes that are so loose that they flop around. If there is a broken spoke, follow the replacement procedure in the following section. If there is a single loose spoke, check to see that the rim is not dented or cracked in that area. I recommend replacing the rim if it is. If the rim looks okay, mark the loose spoke with a piece of tape, and tighten it up with the spoke wrench until it feels the same tension as adjacent spokes on the same side of the wheel (pluck the spoke and listen to the tone). Then follow the truing procedure below.

2. Grab the rim while the wheel is on the bike, and flex it side to side to check the hub bearing adjustment. If the bearings are loose, the wheel will clunk side to side. The hub will need to be tightened before you true the wheel, or the wheel will behave erratically.

3. Put the wheel in a truing stand, if you have one. Otherwise, leave it on the bike. Suspend the bike in a bike stand or from the ceiling, or turn it upside down on the handlebars and saddle.

4. Adjust the truing stand feeler, or hold one of your brake pads so that it scrapes the rim at the biggest wobble.

5. Where the rim scrapes, tighten the

spoke (or spokes) that come(s) to the rim from the opposite side of the hub, and loosen the spoke(s) that come(s) from the same side of the hub as the rim scrapes. This will pull the rim away from the feeler or brake pad.

When correcting a wheel that is laterally out of true (wobbles side-to-side), always tighten spokes in pairs: one spoke coming from one side of the wheel, the other from the opposite side. Tightening spokes is like opening a jar upside down. With the jar right-side up, turning the lid to the left opens the jar, but this reverses when you turn the jar upside down (try it and see). Spoke nipples are just like the lid on that upside-down jar. In other words, when the nipples are at the bottom of the rim, counter-clockwise tightens, and clockwise loosens). The opposite is true when the nipples to be turned are at the top. It may take you a few attempts before you catch on, but you will eventually get it. If

you temporarily make the wheel worse, simply undo what you have done and start over.

It is best to tighten and loosen by small amounts (about a quarter-turn at a time), decreasing the amount you turn the spoke nipples as you move away from the spot where the rim scrapes the hardest. If the wobble gets worse, then you are turning the spokes the wrong direction.

6. As the rim moves more toward center, readjust the truing-stand feeler or the brake pad so that it again finds the most out-of-true spot on the wheel.

7. Check the wobble first on one side of the wheel and then the other, adjusting spokes accordingly, so that you don't end up pulling the whole wheel off center by chasing wobbles only on one side. As the wheel gets closer to true, you will need to decrease the amount you turn the spokes to avoid over-correcting.

8. Accept a certain amount of wobble, especially if truing in a bike, since the

in-the-bike method of wheel truing is not very accurate and is not at all suited for making a wheel absolutely true. If you have access to a wheel-dishing tool, check to make sure that the wheel is centered.

REPLACING A BROKEN SPOKE

Go to the bike store and get a new spoke of the same length. Remember: the spokes on the front wheel are usually not the same length as the spokes on the rear. Also, the spokes on the drive side of the rear wheel are almost always shorter than those on the other side.

1. Make sure you are using the proper thickness and length spoke.
2. Thread the spoke through the spoke hole in the hub flange. If the broken spoke is on the drive side of the rear wheel, you will need to remove the cassette cogs or the freewheel to get at the hub flange.
3. Weave the new spoke in with the other spokes just as it was before. It may take some bending

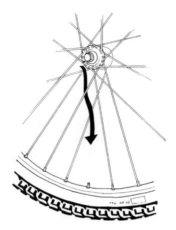

WEAVING A NEW SPOKE

to get it in place.
4. Thread it into the same nipple, if the nipple is in good shape. Otherwise, use a new nipple; you'll need to remove the tire, tube and rim strip to install it.
5. Mark the new spoke with a piece of tape, and tighten it up about as snugly as the neighboring spokes on that side of the wheel.
6. Follow the steps for truing a wheel as outlined above.

HUBS, FREEHUBS AND FREEWHEELS

Hubs are, on occasion, the source of mystery wobbles. If the adjustment is out, the hub shell may be moving back-and-forth on the axle. If that is the case, check with your mechanic or read through a maintenance manual ("Zinn and the Art of Mountain Bike Maintenance," for example) for the step-by-step directions to repair and readjust your hub.

Freehubs and freewheels contain the freewheeling mechanism that allows the bicycle to coast and locks up when pedaling forward. Sprockets (also called "cogs") mount to the freehub or freewheel for the chain to drive.

A freehub is integral with the rear hub, while a freewheel threads onto the outside of the hub shell. Changing gear ratios on a freehub is accomplished by switching cog sets, which slide onto the freehub body along lengthwise grooves (or "splines"). Changing freewheel ratios is done by interchanging the entire freewheel.

Freewheels are almost non-existent on new bikes anymore. The convenience and greater rigidity of freehubs have resulted in an almost complete abandonment of freewheels by the bike industry.

Freewheels and freehubs can stop working if the mechanism inside either will no longer spin forward freely, or the ratchet mechanism will no longer lock up. If a freehub or freewheel needs service, and it is a good idea to clean and lubricate them every year or so even if they are still working fine, you should either have a shop do it

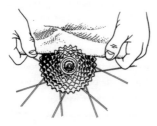

CLEANING COGS

or buy a good bike manual that explains how to service them. "Zinn and the Art of Mountain Bike Maintenance" covers minor lubrication, while "The Mountain Bike Performance Handbook", by Lennard Zinn covers cleaning, heavier lubrication, overhaul and upgrading freehub internals.

<u>CLEANING REAR COGS</u>

The quickest, though perfunctory, way to clean the rear cogs is to slide a

USING CHAIN WHIP

rag back and forth between each pair of cogs. The other way is to remove them and wipe them off with a rag or immerse them in solvent.

<u>CHANGING CASSETTE COGS</u>

1. Get out a chain whip, a cassette lockring remover, a wrench (adjustable or open) to fit the remover, and the cog(s) you want to install. (Some very old cassettes have a threaded smallest cog instead of a lockring. These require two chain whips and no lockring remover.)

2. Remove the skewer.

3. Wrap the chain whip around a cog at least two up from the smallest cog, wrapped in the drive direction to hold the cassette in place.

4. Insert the splined lock-ring remover into the lockring. It is the metallic ring with a splined hole holding the smallest cog in place. Unscrew it in a counterclockwise direction while using the chain whip to keep the cassette from turning. If the lockring is so tight

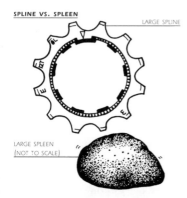

SPLINE VS. SPLEEN

LARGE SPLINE

LARGE SPLEEN
(NOT TO SCALE)

that the tool pops out and damages it, put the skewer through the hub and tool without the springs and tighten it. Loosen the lockring a fraction of a turn, remove the skewer, and unscrew it the rest of the way.

5. Pull the cogs straight off. Some cassette cogsets are all single cogs separated by loose spacers, some cogsets are bolted together, and some are a combination of both.

6. Clean the cogs with a rag or a toothbrush and perhaps some solvent.

7. Inspect the cogs for wear. If the teeth are hook-shaped, they may be ripe for replacement. Rohloff also makes a cog wear indicator tool. If you have access to one, use it following the accompanying instructions.

8. a. If you are replacing the entire cogset, just slide the new one on. Usually, one spline is wider than the others.

b. If you are replacing some individual cogs within your cogset, be certain that they are of the same type and model. For example, not all 16-tooth Shimano cogs are alike. Most cogs have shifting ramps, differentially shaped teeth, and other asymmetries. They differ with model as well as with sizes of the adjacent cogs, so you need to buy one for the exact location and model. Install them in decreasing numerical sequence with the numbers facing out.

Bolt-together cogsets disassembled for cleaning can be put back together or not. There are two kinds of bolt-together cogsets: one with

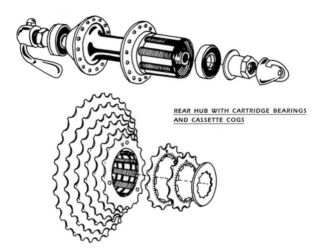

REAR HUB WITH CARTRIDGE BEARINGS AND CASSETTE COGS

three long thin bolts holding the stack of cogs and spacers together, and one with cogs bolted to an aluminum spider that has internal splines to fit on the cassette body. For the type with the three bolts, just unscrew the bolts, take it apart, and put in the replacement cogs.

To save time and trouble with bolt-together cogsets in the future, you can put the cogs back on the cassette body individually and throw out the bolts.

9. Tighten the lockring back on with the lockring remover and wrench. (If you have the old type with the thread-on first cog, tighten that on with a chain whip instead.) Make sure that all of the cogs are seated and can't wobble side to side, which would indicate that the second cog is sitting against the ends of the splines. If they are loose, loosen the lockring, line up the second cog until it falls in place, and tighten the lockring again.

Brakes

"But to come to a stop involved the jamming of myself, molecule by molecule, into whatever lay in my way; meant bringing my atoms into such intimate contact with those of the obstacle that a profound chemical reaction — possibly a far-reaching explosion — would result...."

— "THE TIME MACHINE," H. G. WELLS, 1895

Well, hopefully your local bike shop let you out the door with your brakes working a little better than that. A new bike is usually in perfect working order, but after a few days or weeks, things start settling in, stretching and slipping out of adjustment. The most likely candidates are your brakes. Since they are also the most important component on your bike, you should learn how to make the necessary adjustments to keep them in good shape.

Let's start with one of the most important elements:

CABLES AND HOUSING

Given that cables transfer braking force from the levers to the brakes, their proper installation and maintenance are critical to good brake performance. If there is excess friction in the cable system, the brakes will not work properly, no matter how well the brakes, calipers and levers are adjusted. Each cable should move freely and be replaced if there are any broken strands.

CABLE TENSIONING

As brake pads wear and cables

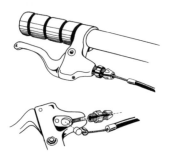

CABLE INSTALLATION AT BRAKE LEVER

stretch, the cable needs to be shortened. The barrel adjuster on the brake lever offers adjustment to mitigate these kind of changes. The cable should be tight enough that the lever cannot be pulled to the grip, yet loose enough that the brakes (assuming they are centered and the wheels are true) are not dragging on the rims.

INCREASING CABLE TENSION

1. Back out the barrel adjuster by turning it counterclockwise, after loosening the locknut.

2. Adjust the tension so that the brake lever does not hit the grip when the

brake is applied. Lock in the tension by tightening the locknut down against the lever body while holding the barrel adjuster.

Note: Some levers, like Shimano's XTR, do not have a locknut on the barrel adjuster.

3. You may find that you need to tighten the cable more than by simply fiddling with the barrel adjuster. If you need to take up more slack than the barrel adjuster allows you to, tighten the cable at the brake. First, screw the barrel adjuster most of the way in. This leaves some adjustment in the system for brake setup and cable stretch over time. Loosen the bolt clamping the cable at the brake. Check the cable for wear. If there are any frayed strands, replace it. Otherwise, pull the cable tight, and re-tighten the clamping bolt. Tension the cable as needed with the barrel adjuster.

REDUCING CABLE TENSION

1. Back out the locknut on the barrel adjuster a few turns

(counterclockwise).

2. Turn the barrel adjuster clockwise until your brake pads are properly spaced from the rim.

3. Tighten the locknut clockwise against the lever body to lock in the adjustment.

4. Double-check that the cable is tight enough so that the lever cannot be squeezed all the way to the grip.

CABLE MAINTENANCE

1. If the cable is frayed or kinked or has any broken strands, replace it.

2. If the cable is not sliding well, lubricate it. If you have it, use molybdenum disulfide grease; otherwise, try a chain lubricant. Standard lithium-based greases can gum up on cables and eventually restrict movement.

3. To lubricate, open the brake.

4. Pull each section of cable housing out of each slotted cable stop. If your bike does not have slotted cable stops, you will have to pull out the entire cable.

5. Slide the housing up the cable, rub lubricant with your fingers on the cable section that was inside the housing, and slide the housing back into place.

6. If the cable still sticks, replace it.

BRAKE LEVERS

To work properly, the levers must operate smoothly and be set so that you can easily reach them while riding.

LEVER LUBRICATION AND SERVICE

1. Lubricate all pivot points in the lever with grease or oil if sticky.

2. Check return spring function for levers that have them.

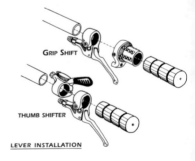

GRIP SHIFT

THUMB SHIFTER

LEVER INSTALLATION

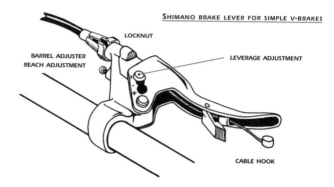

SHIMANO BRAKE LEVER FOR SIMPLE V-BRAKES

LOCKNUT

BARREL ADJUSTER
REACH ADJUSTMENT

LEVERAGE ADJUSTMENT

CABLE HOOK

3. Make sure that the lever or lever body is not bent in a way that hinders movement.

4. Check for stress cracks, and, if you find any, replace the lever.

LEVER REMOVAL, INSTALLATION, AND POSITIONING

Levers mount on the bar inboard of the grip and bar end. They are also mounted inboard of twist shifters and outboard of thumb shifters. Some manufacturers offer integrated systems that include both lever and shifter in a single unit.

1. If installed, remove the bar end by loosening the mounting bolt and sliding it off.

2. Remove the handlebar grip by lifting the edges on both ends, squirting water or rubbing alcohol underneath, and twisting it until it becomes free and slides off.

3. If installed, remove the twist shifter by loosening the mounting bolt and sliding it off.

4. Loosen the brake lever's mounting bolt with an Allen wrench and slide the lever off.

5. Slide the new lever on, and replace the other parts in the order in which they were installed. Slide

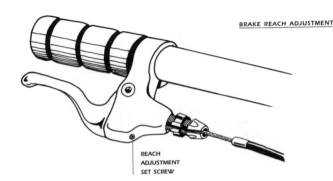

BRAKE REACH ADJUSTMENT

REACH
ADJUSTMENT
SET SCREW

the grips on using rubbing alcohol (it dries quickly) as a lubricant; water works, too, but the grips will twist for a few rides.

6. Make certain the levers do not extend beyond the ends of the bars. Rotate them and slide them inward to your preference.

7. Tighten all mounting bolts on levers, shifters, and bar ends.

Reach and Leverage Adjustments

Some levers have a reach adjustment set screw; usually it's on the lever body just under the barrel adjuster. If you have small hands, you may want to tighten the reach

set screws so the levers are closer to the bars when released.

Some brakes also have a leverage adjustment, which moves the cable end in or out relative to the lever pivot. To adjust the leverage, some levers have a threaded shaft on the cable hook; some have removable inserts; some have adjustable settings of a set screw; others yet use a rotating notched eccentric disc. The closer the cable passes by the pivot, the higher the leverage, but the less cable the lever pulls, and vice versa.

Safety note: The levers for V-

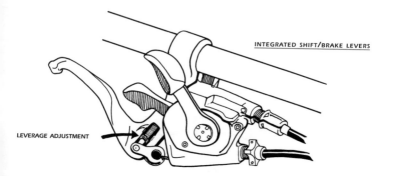

INTEGRATED SHIFT/BRAKE LEVERS

LEVERAGE ADJUSTMENT

brakes have intentionally low leverage (with high cable pull), due to the high leverage of the long brake arms. If you use a lever from a cantilever brake with a V-brake, you can end up on your nose. Always start with V-brake levers adjusted to lowest leverage (cable passing furthest from the lever pivot), and increase from there if you wish.

LEVERAGE ADJUSTMENT

Some levers allow a certain amount of adjustment to vary the distance between the lever pivot and the head of the cable. To start with, set it at the position that offers the weakest leverage, where the head of the cable is farthest from the pivot. Only increase the leverage if you become very confident in using the brakes. On Shimano XTR and Avid, a threaded adjuster performs the adjustment; on Shimano XT, leverage is adjusted by installing or removing a series of inserts; on Shimano DX and M600, leverage is adjusted by loosening a small bolt on the upper face of the lever arm with a 3mm Allen key, sliding the leverage adjuster up and down, and re-tightening the bolt. M600 and DX levers have a hook with a cover to hold the cable end far out at the end of the lever; the cable passes over a grooved trough above the pivot whose height setting determines the leverage.

BRAKE PADS

V-BRAKE PAD REPLACEMENT

Pad replacement on high-end V-brakes with removable pad inserts.
1. With a pair of pliers, remove the cotter pin from the top of the pad holder
2. Slide the old pad out out of its groove in the pad holder.
3. Slide in the new pad, paying attention to the "R" and "L" markings for right and left and the "Forward" direction arrow, if present. Right and left must be heeded, as the backs of these pads only have a slot for the cotter pin on one end. Avid pads have two cotter pin slots and can be oriented either way.

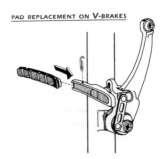

PAD REPLACEMENT ON V-BRAKES

4. Replace the cotter pin, and check that the pad is secure in the holder.
Note: Avid pads are not interchangeable with Shimano XT and XTR, whose pad holders have a curved groove; Avid pad holders have a straight groove, even though the pad itself is curved. The pads are flexible enough that they can be jammed into each other's holders in a pinch, but the outer curvature of the pad will not match that of the rim.

PAD REPLACEMENT ON V-BRAKES WITH ONE-PIECE PAD AND THREADED POST:

1. Note how the washers are stacked on the pad post.

2. Unscrew the shoe fixing nut and remove the old pad from the arm.

3. Replacing the concave and convex washers as they were, bolt the new pad to the arm. The convex washers are placed on either side of the brake arm with flat sides facing in. The concave washers are placed adjacent to the convex washers so that the concave and convex surfaces meet and allow angular adjustability of the pad.

4. Follow pad adjustment procedure above.

CANTILEVER BRAKES

Cantilever brakes are similar to V-brakes in that they have tall arms with pads mounted to them. The brakes are applied by the brake cable pulling up on a yoke (or "straddle cable") connecting the two arms together. This is a less efficient means of pulling the arms together than by using a horizontal section of the brake cable itself, as a V-brake does. Cantilever brake adjustment is usually more compli- cated than with a V-brake. Another disadvantage of cantilevers is that, if the brake cable breaks, the strad- dle cable can fall down on the tire, hook on the knobs, and stop the bike dead.

As a result of these things, the bike industry has abandoned can- tilevers in a span of a couple of short years. If you want to know how to adjust and maintain can- tilevers, consult Zinn and the Art of Mountain Bike Maintenance.

DISC BRAKES

Disc brakes do not use the rims as a braking surface, like most bicy- cle brakes. Instead, a brake disc (or "rotor") is mounted to the hub, like on a car or a motorcycle. Brake pads applied by hydraulic pres- sure, mechanical actuation, or a combination of the two grab the disc to stop the bike. As the weight and reliability of disc brakes for bicycles improves, discs are start- ing to appear as original equip- ment on some mountain bikes.

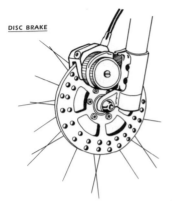

DISC BRAKE

Disc brake calipers (the part with the pistons and brake pads inside) mount to brackets on the left side of the fork and near the left rear dropout of the frame. There is a standard location for these brackets that all disc brake manufacturers except Hayes have agreed upon. Hayes brakes are available with adapters to mount to the standard mounts as well.

Many bicycle disc brakes are "floating caliper" type. These have moving pads on only one side of the disc. The pads on the other side

of the caliper are fixed to the caliper. When the brake is applied, the entire caliper moves laterally to squeeze the rotor between the piston-driven pads and the "anvil" pads (the pads fixed to the caliper). Since the caliper is free to move, exact adjustment of the position of the caliper is not necessary. The brakes always have some "free-running drag", meaning that the rotor is always dragging on the anvil pads, since only the piston-driven pads can retract away from the disc. This drag can be quite severe with some brands, but there is not a lot you can do about it. Making sure that the pins the caliper slides back and forth on are greased will help. Sanding the pads flat will also help, if they are warped on either side.

The other type of disc brake is the "fixed mount" type that has piston-driven pads coming in to the rotor out of either side of the caliper. The position of the caliper must be set very accurately with fixed-mount brakes, since the caliper cannot move, and clearance is small between the pads and rotor. If adjusted correctly, a fixed-mount brake will allow the wheel to spin without drag on the disc, since the pads on either side of the rotor can retract.

Make sure you never squeeze your brake lever when the rotor or a spacer is not in between the brake pads; the pads, and even the pistons on some brakes, can pop out of the calipers. On some brakes, this will require sending it back to the manufacturer to be remedied. Whenever you remove your wheel, it is a good idea to put a spacer as thick as the rotor between the pads. Some brakes come with these spacers. Use them.

Any disc brake has a break-in (or "rotor burnishing") period. You need to slam on the brakes a number of times (perhaps as many as 40 times) before the brakes will come up to full power.

Brake pad replacement is simple with most disc brakes. The pads usually snap in and out easily. Cotter pins and other fixtures must be removed to pull out the pads on some brands, but many require only your fingers to change pads.

On almost any disc brake, the clearance between the pads and the rotor is very small—on the order of .0010 to .0015 inch. This means that any warpage of the rotor will cause brake drag. You should look for this by eyeballing the gap between the rotor and the pads to see if the rotor is warped. If it is, take it to your dealer. Make sure that you protect the rotors whenever you are flying with your bike or shipping it.

Fully hydraulic disc brakes usually come with a bleed kit, and the consumer can shorten or replace hoses, service and bleed the brakes by following the owner's manual. Cable-actuated hydraulic disc brakes have cables and housings connecting the caliper to the brake levers, and only the caliper is hydraulic. Fully mechanical disc brakes are connected to the levers by cables and housings but have mechanical actuation drives the pads. Cable-actuated hydraulic and fully mechanical disc brakes can be serviced from the lever to the caliper like any cable-actuated brake (consult Zinn and the Art of Mountain Bike Maintenance for cable-service procedures). Servicing the inside of the caliper, bleeding, etc., can usually not be done by the consumer on a cable-actuated hydraulic disc brake. Fully mechanical disc brake calipers have no need for bleeding and can sometimes be serviced by the consumer.

Hydraulic Rim Brakes

Hydraulic rim brakes mount onto the same brake posts as V-brakes and cantilevers. There are hydraulic hoses connecting the levers (the "master cylinders") to

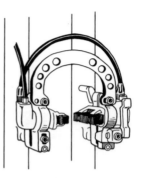

MAGURA HYDRAULIC BRAKE

the calipers, which have slave cylinders pushing pads from either side of the rim. Hydraulic rim brakes are relatively rare, and Magura is the only brand that appears on the market in any significant numbers. The brakes come with a bleed kit for the consumer to bleed the air out of the system. Pad replacement is a snap; the pads pop in and out in seconds by hand.

Zinn and the Art of Mountain Bike Maintenance has a thorough section on servicing Magura hydraulic rim brakes.

Pedals

CHAPTER 8

"It may be uphill pedalling at first…He was a long time before he got to the top. But he got there."

— "A PORTRAIT OF THE ARTIST AS A YOUNG MAN," JAMES JOYCE, 1916

Your legs, lungs and heart are the true source of power on your bicycle. It's just that without the pedals, all that energy would never get to the drivetrain. Obvious as that is, it's important to remember that point when working on your bike.

To transmit power most efficiently, it is important to keep your feet firmly attached to the pedal, either by the old-fashioned strap and toe clip method, or by means of more modern clip-in pedals, which use a cleat to lock your foot down. Beyond that, the measure of a good pedal is whether or not it releases your foot when you need it to. So, if you are using clip-in pedals, be sure to pay close attention to the section on adjusting release-tension, at the end of this chapter.

PEDAL REMOVAL AND INSTALLATION

Before you do anything to your pedals, remember that the right

REMOVING PEDAL WITH 15MM WRENCH

REMOVING PEDAL WITH A 6MM ALLEN WRENCH

pedal axle is right-hand threaded and the left is left-hand (reverse) threaded. Both unscrew from the crank in the pedaling direction.

REMOVAL

1. Slide the 15mm pedal wrench onto the wrench flats of the pedal axle. Or, if the pedal axle is designed to accept it, you can use a 6mm Allen wrench from the back side of the crank arm. This is particularly handy on the trail, since you probably won't be carrying a 15mm wrench anyway. But, if you are at home and the pedal is on really tight, it'll probably be easier to use the standard pedal wrench. Some pedals, like the Time ATAC and Time TMT, have no wrench flats and can only be removed with a 6mm Allen wrench.

2. Unscrew the pedal in the appropriate direction. The right, or drive-side, pedal unscrews counterclockwise when viewed from that side. The left-side pedal is reverse threaded, so it unscrews in a clockwise direction when viewed from the left side of the bike. Once loosened, either pedal can be unscrewed quickly by turning the crank forward with the wrench engaged on the pedal spindle.

INSTALLATION

1. Use a rag to wipe the threads clean on the pedal axle and inside the crankarm.

2. Grease the pedal threads.

3. Start screwing the pedal in with your fingers, clockwise for the right pedal, counterclockwise for the left.

4. Tighten the pedal with the 15mm pedal wrench or a 6mm Allen wrench. This can be done quickly by turning the cranks backward with the wrench engaged on the pedal spindle.

TYPES OF PEDALS

PLATFORM

Simple platform pedals are still fairly common on lower-end bikes. They are relatively unintimidating for the novice rider, and the frame (or "cage") that surrounds the pedal provides a large, stable platform. Without a toeclip, the top and bottom of the pedal are the same and you can use just about any type of shoe. If you mount a toeclip without a strap, it can keep your foot from sliding forward and still allow easy release in almost any direction. When you add a toe strap and cleats, the combination works well to keep your foot on the pedal while riding even the roughest of single track. When tightened, the strap allows you to pull up on the

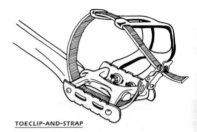

TOECLIP-AND-STRAP

upward part of the pedal stroke — giving you more power and a more fluid pedal stroke. Of course, as you add clips and straps, the pedal becomes harder to enter and exit, and boots or shoes with aggressive tread designs become increasingly difficult to use.

CLIP-IN MODELS

Clip-in pedals offer all of the advantages of a good clip-and-strap combination, yet allow easy entry and exit from the pedal. These pedals are more expensive and require special shoes and accurate mounting of the cleats. Your choice of shoes is limited to stiff-sole models that accept cleats for your particular

CLIP-IN PEDAL

pedal. Once you have them dialed in, you will find that clip-in pedals waste less energy through flex and slippage and allow you to transfer more power directly to the pedals. This greater efficiency explains their almost universal acceptance among cross-country mountain-bike racers. Most clip-in mountain pedals are "SPD" style; SPD stands for Shimano Pedaling Dynamics, as Shimano was the originator of the first successful clip-in mountain pedal in the mid-1980s. "SPD-compatibility, "shared by virtually all current clip-in mountain pedals, indicates that the cleat mounts with two side-by-side 5mm x 0.8mm-thread screws, spaced 14mm apart,

screwing into a movable threaded cleat-mounting plate on a shoe with two longitudinal grooves in the sole. It does not mean that one company's cleat will necessarily work with the pedal of another company.

SETTING UP CLIP-IN PEDALS

Setting up clip-in pedals involves installation and adjustment of the cleats on the shoes, and adjusting the pedal-release tension.

INSTALLING AND ADJUSTING PEDAL CLEATS ON THE SHOES

The cleat is important because its position determines the fore-aft, lateral (side-to-side) and rotational position of your foot. If your pedals aren't properly oriented, it could eventually cause hip, knee or ankle problems.

1. If your shoe has a pre-cut piece of rubber covering the cleat-mounting area, remove it. Cut around the cover's outline with a knife, pry an edge up with a screwdriver, and yank it off with some pliers. Warming it up with a hair dryer beforehand softens the glue.

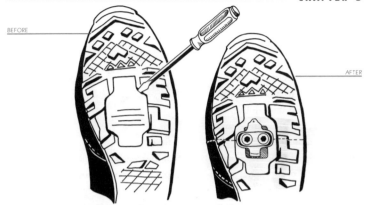

BEFORE

AFTER

SETTING UP CLEATS ON A SPD-COMPATIBLE SHOE

2. Put the shoe on, and mark the position of the ball of your foot (the big bump behind your big toe) on the outside of the shoe. This will help you position the cleat so the ball of your foot will be over the pedal spindle. Take the shoe off, and continue drawing the line straight across the bottom of the shoe.

3. If there are threaded holes in your shoe sole to accept the cleat screws, skip to step 4. If you do not have threaded shoe holes, you must install the backing plate and thread-

ed cleat plate that came with your pedals. Remove the shoe's sock liner, put the rectangular backing plate inside the shoe over the two holes, and put the threaded plate on top of it.

4. Lube the cleat screw threads, and screw the cleat that came with your pedals to your shoe; this usually requires a 4mm Allen wrench. Make sure you orient the cleat in the appropriate direction. Some cleats have an arrow indicating forward; if yours do not, the instructions

accompanying your pedals probably specify which direction the cleat should point.

5. Position the cleat in the middle of its lateral- and rotational-adjustment range, and line up the mounting screws over the mark you made in Step 2.

Note: Cleats for Time ATAC pedals have no lateral or rotational adjustment; just set the screws at your mark and tighten the cleat down, making sure the arrow on the cleat points forward. Put the cleat with the imprinted stars onto the right shoe for more float range; put it on the left shoe for less float. You may now tighten the screws, skip the remaining steps and go riding! (Incidentally, the older model Time TMT pedal, of which few were sold, also is set up the same way — with only fore-aft cleat adjustment, but the only shoe you could use with it was Time's mountain shoe of the time. The newer ATAC works with any SPD-compatible shoe.)

TIME A.T.A.C.

6. Snug the screws down enough that the cleat won't move when clipped in or out of the pedals, but don't tighten them down fully yet. Follow the same steps with your other shoe.

7. In order to set the lateral position, put the shoes on, sit on the bike, and clip into the pedals. Ride around a bit. Notice the position of your feet. Pedaling is more efficient the closer the feet are to the plane of the bike, but you don't want them in so far that they bump your cranks. Take the shoes off and adjust the cleats laterally, if necessary, to move the feet side to side. Get back on the bike and clip in again.

8. In order to set the rotational position, ride around some more. Notice

if your feet feel twisted and uncomfortable. You may feel pressure on either side of your heel from the shoe. If necessary, remove your shoes and rotate the cleat slightly. Some pedals offer free-float, allowing the foot to rotate freely for a few degrees before releasing. Precise rotational cleat adjustment is less important if the pedal is free-floating.

SPEEDPLAY FROG

Note: On Speedplay Frogs, angle the cleat slightly toward the outside of the shoe, and tighten the mounting screws just enough that the cleat can still turn. Clip into the pedal and rotate the heel inward until it just touches the crankarm. Tighten the cleat in this position (Frogs have no inward release; this sets the inward stop).

9. Once your cleat position feels right, trace the cleats with a pen so that you can tell if the cleat stays put. While holding the cleat in place, tighten the bolts down firmly. Hold the Allen wrench close to the bend so that you do not exert too much lever-age and strip the bolts.

10. If the cleat holes are open to the inside of the shoe, place a waterproof sticker over the opening inside, and replace the sock liner.

11. When riding, bring the 4mm Allen wrench along, since you may want to fine-tune this adjustment over the course of a few rides.

ADJUSTING RELEASE-TENSION ON CLIP-IN PEDALS

If you find the factory release-adjustment setting to be too loose or too restrictive, you can adjust the release tension on most clip-in pedals; exceptions are Time and Speedplay. The adjusting screws are

3MM ALLEN WRENCH

usually located at the front and rear of the pedal. The screws affect the tension of the nearest set of clips. The adjusters are usually operated with a small (usually 3mm) Allen wrench. The old-style Onza and Look SL3 pedals use slightly different adjustment methods. The manufacturer's instructions for those

LOOK SL-3

are included with the pedals or are described in a more detailed maintenance manual.

1. Locate the tension-adjustment screws. They are usually on either fore and aft end of the pedal.

2. To loosen the tension-adjustment, turn the screw counterclockwise, and to tighten it, turn it clockwise. It's the classic "lefty loosey, righty tighty" approach. There usually are click stops in the rotation of the screw. Tighten or loosen one click at a time (one-quarter to one-half turn), and go riding to test the adjustment. Many types include an indicator that moves with the screw to show relative adjustment. Make certain that you do not back the screw out so far that it comes out of the spring plate.

Note: With Ritchey, Scott, Girvin, Topo, Wellgo and other dual-rear-clip/dual-rear-spring pedals, you will decrease the amount of free-float in the pedal as you increase the release tension.

CHAPTER 9
Forks and headsets

"If you come to a fork in the road, take it."

— YOGI BERRA

THE IMPORTANCE OF BEING THOROUGH

Okay, okay… so far, we've said that the drive train, the pedals and frame are the most critical parts of the bike. All of that's true, but when it comes to making sure that there is *one* part of your bike that you can not afford to have fail, it has to be your fork.

The bad news is that the world is full of horror stories of the disastrous consequences of any variety of fork failures. There is no need to go into detail. Imagination should suffice. The good news is that almost without exception, these disasters can be avoided. Inspect, inspect and inspect. And if you are using a suspension fork,

inspect some more. Always check your fork for cracks, bends, ripples or anything that might be considered unusual. Make sure that the headset is properly adjusted. Make certain that the stem is properly attached, but not over-tightened. When in doubt, don't ride it, get an expert to check it. Always, always, always err on the side of caution.

That said, let's go through the steps you can take to ensure that your fork and bike work properly.

SUSPENSION FORKS

The suspension fork will provide a more comfortable ride, better handling and access to higher speeds on rough terrain. It will do

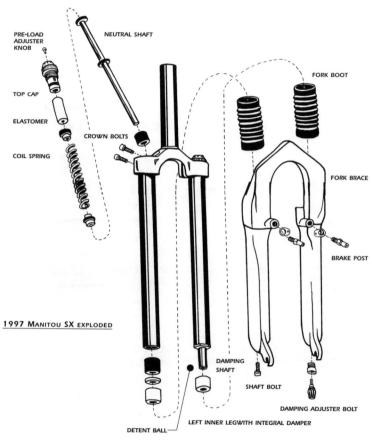

PRE-LOAD
ADJUSTER
KNOB

NEUTRAL SHAFT

FORK BOOT

TOP CAP

ELASTOMER

CROWN BOLTS

COIL SPRING

FORK BRACE

BRAKE POST

1997 MANITOU SX EXPLODED

DAMPING
SHAFT

SHAFT BOLT

DAMPING ADJUSTER BOLT

DETENT BALL

LEFT INNER LEG WITH INTEGRAL DAMPER

this for many years, provided you keep it in good running order.

CHECKING THE CONDITION OF YOUR SUSPENSION FORK

A telescoping suspension fork must be well-lubricated in order to slide smoothly up and down. You can extend the life of the fork and maximize the interval between lubrications by keeping fork boots on your fork. The boots are rubber accordion-like tubes that fit on the inner legs of the fork. Make sure that your fork has them, and check them frequently to assure that the bottom of the boots are fitted tightly around the top of the fork's outer legs. The boot snaps into a groove around the top edge of the inner leg.

You can determine your fork's need for service with a simple test. Stand next to the bike and grab the handlebar grips. Squeeze the front brake and push down on the handlebars. Gradually increase the pressure down on the bars. The

ADJUSTING SPRING PRE-LOAD

fork should start to slide in smoothly and should continue to move smoothly down as you increase the downward force. If it takes a lot of force to get the fork to move initially, and then it moves down in a chunk-chunk-chunk stair-step fashion, then the fork needs lubrication.

The inner legs slide through cylindrical bushings in the outer legs. If the bushings and the inner legs are too dry, they will not slide smoothly.

Lubricating the fork requires disassembling it, cleaning it, and lubricating the inner legs and the

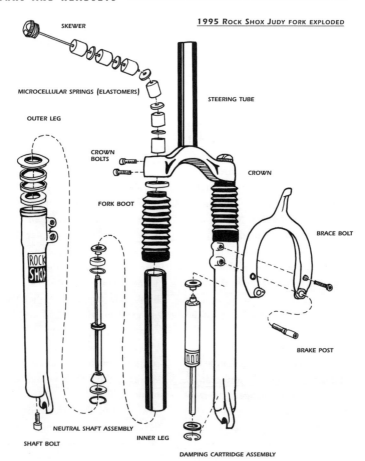

SKEWER

1995 ROCK SHOX JUDY FORK EXPLODED

MICROCELLULAR SPRINGS (ELASTOMERS)

STEERING TUBE

OUTER LEG

CROWN BOLTS

CROWN

FORK BOOT

BRACE BOLT

ROCK SHOX

BRAKE POST

NEUTRAL SHAFT ASSEMBLY

INNER LEG

SHAFT BOLT

DAMPING CARTRIDGE ASSEMBLY

bushings inside the outer legs with grease. The exception to this are forks that have grease ports on the outer legs that can be lubricated from the outside with a grease gun. Cleaning and lubricating a suspension fork is covered in Chapter 11 of "Zinn and the Art of Mountain Bike Maintenance," if you wish to do it yourself. Otherwise, take the fork to a shop for service.

Service the fork frequently, erring on the side of too frequently. If you let it go too long, grit will scratch the surface of the inner legs and grind out the inside diameter of the bushings. The rough inner legs will never slide smoothly again. If the bushings get too worn, the fork will be loose; the inner legs will clunk back and forth inside the outer legs as you push the bike back and forth with the front brake on. You will have to take it to a shop to get the bushings replaced.

TUNING COIL SPRING/ELASTOMER FORKS

SETTING SPRING PRELOAD

Spring preload can be adjusted on most mid- to high-end coil spring/elastomer forks. Preload determines the way a spring responds to the forces applied to it. On a coil spring/elastomer fork, you can adjust the preload simply by turning the adjuster knobs on the top of the fork crown. With most forks, you can adjust the preload while riding, as you encounter terrain variations.

Rotating the adjuster knobs clockwise gives a firmer ride by tightening down on (and thus shortening) the spring stack. Rotating the adjuster knobs counterclockwise softens the ride. Make sure the top cap surrounding the knob does not unscrew from the fork crown; you may need to hold it tight with one hand (or a wrench) when you loosen the adjuster knob. Check the top cap occasionally to make sure it is not unscrewed or being forced out due to stripped threads. If its threads seem to be stripped, get a new top cap right away, before you ride any more; if the top cap pops off, the spring can shoot up into your face at high velocity.

Preloading the springs does not limit the full travel for large bumps; it alters the force required to initially move the springs when you encounter smaller bumps. Varying the preload also changes the fork's sag.

FINE TUNING DAMPING

Some high-end elastomer forks have a hydraulic damping cartridge or cylinder inside one or both lower legs. Most elastomer forks do not have these (if there is no bolt at the bottom of the fork legs, it does not have one). Of those with damping cartridges, not all are adjustable (for example, the cartridges on the earliest Judy XCs were not adjustable).

Manitou Mach 5, SX, SX-Ti and EFC and 1996 and later Rock Shox Judy forks (all models) have adjustable damping.

Rebound damping controls the speed at which the fork returns to its original position after it has been compressed and released.

Compression damping controls the speed at which the spring compresses during the fork's downstroke.

On a Manitou Mach 5, SX, SX-Ti or EFC, the rebound damping is adjustable via a knob at the bottom of the left leg. The Mach 5,SX,SX-Ti rebound damping adjuster knob is tall and made of black plastic; the EFC knob is flat and aluminum. Turning the knob clockwise increases rebound damping (and slows the return stroke), and counterclockwise decreases rebound damping. It is not recommended to ride with full damping, as it will almost prevent the fork from returning

2MM ALLEN WRENCH

ADJUSTING DAMPING ON ROCK SHOX JUDY FORK

DAMPING ADJUSTER KNOB ON MANITOU

after compression. Compression damping in these Manitou forks can only be changed by varying the shim stack inside the damping unit; see your owner's manual.

On all pre-1997 adjustable Rock Shox Judy models, the compression damping is adjusted by inserting a 2mm hex key through the center of the hollow shaft bolt at the bottom of the left leg. Clockwise rotation increases compression damping. All 1997 models have an optional knurled aluminum knob inserted inside the bottom leg bolt, like Manitou; compression damping is adjusted by turning the knob or, in the absence of the knob, by turning a 3mm Allen key inserted through the bottom bolt.

Only Judy DH and DHO forks (the red ones) include an additional adjustable cartridge in the right leg to control rebound damping. It can also be adjusted with a 2mm hex key on a DH through the center of the hollow shaft bolt on the bottom of the right fork leg and on the DHO with a 3mm Allen key or an optional knob. Clockwise rotation increases rebound damping (slows the return stroke). It is very important that you do not turn this adjuster any more than

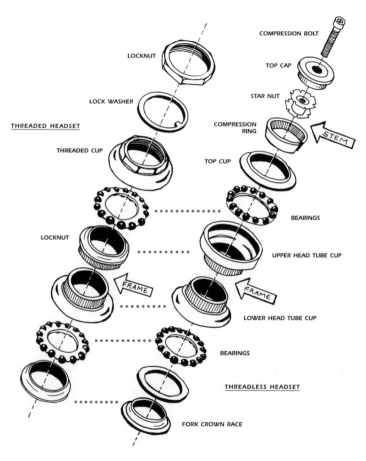

COMPRESSION BOLT

TOP CAP

STAR NUT

LOCKNUT

LOCK WASHER

THREADED HEADSET

THREADED CUP

COMPRESSION RING

STEM

TOP CUP

BEARINGS

LOCKNUT

UPPER HEAD TUBE CUP

FRAME

FRAME

LOWER HEAD TUBE CUP

BEARINGS

THREADLESS HEADSET

FORK CROWN RACE

two full turns counterclockwise!

The 1998 Manitou forks will have no springs in the left leg, only a "twin piston" damper adjustable for compression damping at the top and rebound damping at the bottom. All of the springs will be in the right leg.

Marzocchi Bombers also have damping adjusters on the bottom of the leg.

HEADSETS

ADJUSTING A THREADED HEADSET

The secret to good adjustment is simultaneously controlling the steering tube, the adjustable cup and the locknut as you tighten the latter two together.

Note: Perform the adjustment with the stem installed. Not only does it give you something to hold onto that keeps the fork from turning during the installation, but there are slight differences in adjustment when the stem is in place as opposed to

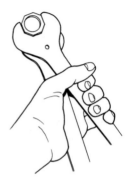

TIGHTENING HEADSET LOCKNUT

when it is not. Tightening the stem bolt can sometimes bulge the walls of the steering tube very slightly, but just enough for it to shorten the steering tube and throw your original headset adjustment off.

1. Follow the steps outlined in Chapter 2, and determine whether the headset is too loose or too tight.

2. Put a pair of headset wrenches that fit your headset on the headset's top nut (also called the "locknut") and top bearing cup

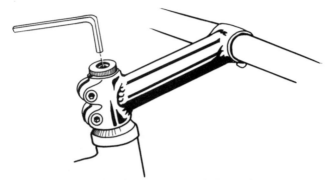

LOOSENING AND TIGHTENING BOLT ON THREADLESS-STYLE HEADSET

(or "threaded cup" or "adjustable cup"). Headset nuts come in a wide variety of sizes, so make sure you have purchased the proper size wrench. Place the wrenches so that the top one is slightly offset to left of the bottom wrench. That way you can squeeze them together to free the nut.

Note: People with small hands or weak grip will need to grab each wrench out at the end to get enough leverage.

3. Hold the lower wrench in place and turn the top wrench counter-clockwise about a quarter-turn to loosen the locknut. It may take considerable force to break it loose, since it needs to be installed very tightly to keep the headset from loosening up.

4. If the headset was too loose, turn the lower (or threaded) cup clockwise about 1/16 of a turn while holding the stem with your other hand. Be very careful when tightening the cup; over-tightening it can ruin the headset by pressing the bearings into the bearing surfaces and making lit-

tle indentations. The headset then stops at the indentations rather than turns smoothly, a condition known as a "pitted" headset.

If the headset was too tight, loosen the threaded cup counter-clockwise 1/16 turn while holding the stem with your other hand. Loosen it until the bearings turn freely, but be sure not to loosen it to the point that you allow any play to develop.

5. Holding the stem, tighten the locknut clockwise with a single wrench. Make sure that the threaded cup does not turn while you tighten the locknut. If it does turn, you either are missing the toothed lock washer separating the cup and locknut, or the washer you have is missing its tooth. In this case, remove the locknut and replace the toothed washer. Put it on the steering tube so that the tooth engages the longitudinal groove in the steering tube. Tighten the locknut on again.

Note: You can adjust a headset without a toothed washer by working both wrenches simultaneously, but it is trickier and the headset often comes loose while riding.

6. Check the headset adjustment again. Repeat steps 4 and 5 until properly adjusted.

7. Once properly adjusted, place one wrench on the locknut and the other on the threaded cup. Tighten the locknut (clockwise) firmly against the washer(s) and threaded cup to hold the headset adjustment in place.

8. Check the headset adjustment again. If it is off, follow steps 2-7 again. If it is adjusted properly, make sure the stem is aligned with the front wheel, and go ride your bike.

Note: If you constantly get what you believe to be the proper adjustment, and then find it to be too loose after you tighten the locknut and threaded cup against each other, the steering tube may be too long, causing the locknut to bottom out. Remove the stem and examine the inside of the steering tube. If the top end of the steering tube butts up against the top lip of the locknut, the steering tube is too long. Remove the locknut and add another spacer.

If you don't want to add another spacer, file off 1or 2mm of the steering tube. Be sure to deburr it inside and out, and avoid leaving filings in the bearings or steering tube threads. Replace the locknut and return to step 5.

Another note: Wheels Manufacturing makes a headset locknut called the "Growler." It replaces the locknut and will not come loose, even on bumpy terrain. It threads on just like a normal locknut and is adjusted the same way. The only difference between a Growler and a standard locknut is that the Growler is split down one side and has a pinch bolt bridging the split.

Once the headset is adjusted, tighten the pinch bolt to keep it in adjustment.

ADJUSTING A THREADLESS HEADSET

Adjusting a threadless headset is much easier than adjusting a threaded one and it usually takes only one tool: a 5mm Allen wrench.

1. Check the headset adjustment. Determine whether the headset is too tight or too loose.

2. Loosen the bolt(s) that clamp the stem to the steering tube.

3. If the headset is too tight, loosen the 5mm Allen bolt on the top cap about 1/16 of a turn.

If the headset is too loose, tighten the 5mm Allen bolt on the top cap about 1/16 of a turn. Be careful not to over-tighten it and pit the headset. If you're using a torque wrench, Dia-Compe recommends a tightening torque on this bolt of 22 inch-pounds.

4. Re-tighten the stem clamp bolt(s).

CHAPTER 10
Stuff at the back of the book

"That lucid and admirable statement seems to be the last word in the matter."

— "THE LOST WORLD," SIR ARTHUR CONAN DOYLE, 1912

KEEPING TRACK

A bike is a complicated piece of equipment with a myriad of interacting parts. One way to ensure that those parts keep working properly is to make certain that your bike is regularly maintained. To do that, you need to keep track of when regular maintenance has been performed. It makes sense to keep all of that information in one place.

Start by recording the date and place of purchase and serial numbers of all original equipment on the bike that can be recorded. Keep a record of the parts you have replaced. At the back of the book, we've included a pocket to keep receipts and warranty information.

There is also a spot to keep track of your overall mileage to make certain that you know just how long you've been using a particular part.

BRAND/SIZE/STYLE	PLACE OF PURCHASE	DATE OF PURCHASE	SERIAL NUMBER

BIKE 1
.... 2

FORK 1
.... 2

STEM 1
.... 2

HANDLEBAR 1
.... 2

BAR ENDS 1
.... 2

BRAKES 1
.... 2

SHIFTERS 1
.... 2

DERAILLEURS 1
.... 2

CRANK ARMS 1
.... 2

CHAIN RINGS 1
.... 2

CHAIN 1
.... 2

PEDALS 1
.... 2

RIMS 1
.... 2

HUBS 1
.... 2

TIRES 1
.... 2

SEAT POST 1
.... 2

SADDLE 1
.... 2

ADDITIONAL COMPONENT PURCHASES

	BRAND/SIZE/STYLE	PLACE OF PURCHASE	DATE OF PURCHASE	SERIAL NUMBER
FORK				
STEM				
HANDLEBAR				
BAR ENDS				
BRAKES				
SHIFTERS				
DERAILLEURS				
CRANKARMS				
CHAIN RINGS				
CHAIN				
PEDALS				
HUBS				
CASSETTE				
RIMS				
TIRES				
SEAT POST				
SADDLE				
COMPUTER				
LIGHTS				
RACKS				
NOTE				

SUGGESTED MAINTENACE

<u>EVERY RIDE:</u>

a. Check tire pressure and examine tires

b. Check your brakes

c. Inspect your fork for cracks, bulges, bends etc.

d. Check the stem and bars for the same

<u>EVERY TWO WEEKS OR EVERY 150 MILES:</u>

a. Lubricate chain (more often if you live in an extremely wet or dusty environment)

b. Check brake pad wear

c. Check headset adjustment

d. Do a complete visual inspection, check for loose pedals, look for cracks, dents and dings in your frame and keep an eye open for loose or missing bolts and frayed cables.

e. Inspect wheels for trueness

MAINTENANCE LOG
ENTER DATE MAINTENANCE TO BE PERFORMED

FORK													
BRAKES													
BRAKE PADS													
BRAKE CABLES													
SHIFTERS													
DERAILLEURS													
DERAILLEUR CABLES													
CRANKARMS													
CHAIN													
CHAIN RINGS													
PEDALS													
HUBS													
TIRES													
COMPUTER BATTERY													

SCHEDULE

a. Replace chain

b. Lubricate cables and housing (replace if necessary)

c. Check chainring and cog wear (be certain that your gears don't skip after chain replacement).

d. Overhaul suspension fork.

e. Overhaul suspension seatpost or rear suspension

f. Check rims or disc rotor for braking surface wear and replace if necessary

g. Check the bottom bracket, headset and hub adjustment (overhaul if necessary)

h. Check derailleur adjustment; remove, clean and lube jockey wheels

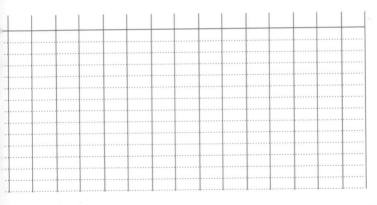

MAINTENANCE NOTES

part	when	what

CULTIVATE A GOOD RELATIONSHIP WITH A SHOP

Keeping your bike in good working order, even if you do the service yourself, will require having a shop or two that you count on fork parts, advice and service. Find a shop that you like whose employees you trust and can talk to easily. Give the shop your business, so that the trusting relationship becomes mutual.

part	when	what

A good dealer not only has tools, parts and materials that you may want, but its people have access to knowledge that will be harder for you to come by. For instance, if there are manufacturer recalls in effect on any of your equipment, your shop will have been alerted and can warn you before you have a problem.

MILEAGE LOG

Date							
FRAME							
FORK							
STEM							
HANDLEBAR							
BAR ENDS							
BRAKES							
BRAKE PADS							
BRAKE CABLES							
SHIFTERS							
DERAILLEURS							
DERAILLEUR CABLES							
CHAIN							
CRANK ARMS							
CRANK RINGS							
PEDALS							
RIMS							
HUBS							
TIRES							
SEAT POST							
SADDLE							
TIRES							

COMPUTER INFO

When you buy a bike computer, the owner's manual contains lots of vital information. No matter how hard you try, you will lose that piece of paper. Use this space to record the following — battery type and size and wheel diameter configuration codes. Be sure to record the formula for calculating codes for various wheel and tire sizes, especially if you have more than one bike.

BATTERY TYPE AND SIZE

**SETTINGS FOR
WHEELSET 1**

WHEELSET 2

FORMULA

STUFF YOU'LL FORGET
UNLESS YOU WRITE IT DOWN HERE

TOP AND SEAT TUBE LENGTHS

FORK TRAVEL

STEM LENGTH AND RISE

HANDLEBAR WIDTH

DISTANCE FROM PEDAL AXLE TO TOP OF SEAT

DISTANCE FROM SEAT FRONT TO STEM

HEIGHT OF SEAT ABOVE STEM

SEAT POST DIAMETER

STEERER TUBE DIAMETER

SPOKE LENGTHS: FRONT

       REAR DRIVE SIDE   REAR NON-DRIVE SIDE

FIRST UCI MOUNTAIN BIKE WORLD CHAMPIONSHIP WINNER

          FOR XC

          FOR DH

MY FAVOURITE COLOR IS

THE INGREDIENTS OF SPAM ARE

GRIPE SHEET

ride/problem	fix now	fix later

brake lever clamp bolt	.52-69 inch-pounds
	(22-26 inch-pounds for slotted screw type)
brake pivot bolt	.43-61 inch-pounds
brake cable fixing bolt	.52-69 inch-pounds
V-brake pad fixing bolt	.52-69 inch-pounds
canti brake pad fixing bolt	.70-78 inch-pounds
straddle cable yoke fixing nut	.35-43 inch-pounds
front derailleur cable fixing bolt	.43-61 inch-pounds
front derailleur clamp bolt	.43-61 inch-pounds
rear derailleur cable fixing bolt	.35-52 inch-pounds
rear derailleur dropout mounting bolt	.70-86 inch-pounds
rear derailleur pulley center bolts	.27-34 inch-pounds
thumb shifter clamp bolt	.53-69 inch-pounds
	(22-26 inch-pounds for slotted screw type)
shift lever parts fixing screw	.22-24 inch-pounds
Gripshift lever mounting screw	.17 inch-pounds
hub quick-release lever closing	.79-104 inch-pounds
quick-release axle locknut	.87-217 inch-pounds
freehub cassette body fixing bolt	.305-434 inch-pounds
cassette cog lockring	.260-434 inch-pounds
crank arm fixing bolt	.357-435 inch-pounds
chainring fixing bolt	.70-95 inch-pounds
cartridge bottom bracket cups	.435-608 inch-pounds
standard bottom bracket fixed cup	.609-695 inch-pounds
standard bottom bracket lockring	.609-695 inch-pounds
pedal axle	.307 inch-pounds or more
seatpost clamp bolt	.174-347 inch-pounds
stem handlebar clamping bolt	.174-260 inch-pounds
stem expander bolt	.174-260 inch-pounds
AheadSet stem clamp bolts	.130 inch-pounds
Aheadset bearing preload	.22 inch-pounds
Rock Shox fork crown clamp bolt	.60 inch-pounds
Rock Shox brake post	.60 inch-pounds
Rock Shox fork brace bolt	.60 inch-pounds
Rock Shox Judy cartridge shaft bolt	.60 inch-pounds
Rock Shox Judy neutral shaft bolt	.60 inch-pounds
Manitou fork crown clamp bolt	.110-130 inch-pounds
Manitou brake post	.90-110 inch-pounds
Manitou fork brace bolt	.90-110 inch-pounds
Manitou EFC/Mach 5 cartridge bolt	.10-30 inch-pounds
Manitou neutral shaft bolt	.10-30 inch-pounds
Manitou EFC/Mach 5 cartridge cap	.30-50 inch-pounds
shoe cleat fixing bolt	.44-51 inch-pounds
shoe spike	.34 inch-pounds

GLOSSARY

adjustable cup: The non-drive side cup in the bottom bracket. This cup is removed for maintenance of the bottom-bracket spindle and bearings, and it adjusts the bearings. Term sometimes applied to top headset cup as well.

AheadSet: a style of headset that allows the use of a fork with a threadless steering tube.

Allen key (Allen wrench, hex key): a hexagonal wrench that fits inside the head of the bolt.

all-terrain bike (ATB): another term for mountain bike.

anchor bolt ("cable anchor", "cable-fixing bolt"): a bolt securing a cable to a component.

axle: the shaft about which a part turns, usually on bearings or bushings.

axle overlock dimension: the length of a hub axle from dropout to dropout, referring to the distance from locknut face to locknut face.

barrel adjuster: a threaded cable stop that allows for fine adjustment of cable tension. Barrel adjusters are commonly found on rear derailleurs, shifters and brake levers.

BB: (see "bottom bracket".)

binder bolt: a bolt clamping a seatpost in a frame, a bar end to a handlebar, a handlebar inside a stem, or a threadless steering tube inside a stem clamp.

bottom bracket (BB): the assembly that allows the crank to rotate. Generally the bottom bracket assembly includes bearings, an axle, a fixed cup, adjustable cup, and a lockring.

bottom-bracket shell: the cylindrical

housing at the bottom of a bicycle frame through which the bottom-bracket axle passes.

brake boss (brake post or pivot; cantilever boss, post, or pivot): a fork- or frame-mounted pivot for a brake arm.

brake pad (brake block): a block of rubber or similar material used to slow the bike by creating friction on the rim or other braking surface.

brake post: (see "brake boss".)

brake shoe: the metal pad holder that holds the brake pad to the brake arm.

braze-on: a generic term for most metal frame attachments, even those welded or glued on.

brazing: a method commonly used to construct steel bicycle frames. Brazing involves the use of brass or silver solder to connect frame tubes and attach various "braze-on" items including brake bosses, cable guides and rack mounts to the frame.

bushing: a metal or plastic sleeve that acts as a simple bearing on pedals, suspension forks, suspension swing arms, and jockey wheels.

butted tubing: a common type of frame tubing with varying wall thicknesses. Butted tubing is designed to accommodate high stress points at the ends of the tube by being thicker there.

cable (inner wire): wound or braided wire strands used to operate brakes and derailleurs.

cable anchor: (see "anchor bolt".)

cable end: a cap on the end of a cable to keep it from fraying.

cable-fixing bolt: (see "anchor bolt".)

cable hanger: cable stop on a fork- or

seatstay-arch used to stop the brake cable housing for a cantilever or U-brake.

cable housing: a metal-reinforced exterior sheath through which a cable passes.

cable housing stop: (see "cable stop".) cable-fixing bolt: an anchor bolt that attaches cables to brakes or derailleurs.

cable stop: a fitting on the frame, fork, or stem at which a cable housing segment terminates.

cage: two guiding plates through which the chain travels. Both the front and rear derailleurs have cages. The cage on the rear also holds the jockey pulleys.

cantilever boss: (see "brake boss".)

cantilever brake: a brake that relies on tension in a straddle cable to move two opposing arms, pivoting on frame- or fork-mounted posts, toward the braking surface of the rim. Cantilevers are one of the most common brake found on mountain bikes.

cantilever pivot: (see "brake boss".)

cantilever post: (see "brake boss".)

cartridge bearing: ball bearings encased in a cartridge consisting of steel inner and outer rings, ball retainers, and, sometimes, bearing covers.

cassette hub: a rear hub that has a built-in freewheel mechanism.

chain: a series of metal links held together by pins and used to transmit energy from the crank to the rear wheel.

chain line: the imaginary line connecting the center of the middle chainring with the middle of the cogset. This line should in theory be straight and parallel with the vertical plane passing through the center of the bicycle. This is measured as the distance from the center of the seat tube to the center of the middle chainring (an easy way to measure this is to measure from the left side of the seat tube to the outside of the large chainring, measure the distance from the right side of the seat tube to the inside of the inner chainring, add these two measurements, and divide the sum by two).

chain link: a single unit of bicycle chain consisting of four plates with a roller on each end and in the center.

chainring: a multiple tooth sprocket attached to the right crankarm.

chainstays: the tubes leading from the bottom bracket shell to the rear hub axle.

chain suck: the dragging of the chain by the chainring past the release point at the bottom of the chainring. The chain can be dragged upward until it is jammed between the chainring and the chainstay.

chainring-nut spanner: a tool used to secure the chainring nuts while tightening the chainring bolts.

chain whip (chain wrench): a flat piece of steel, usually attached to two lengths of chain. This tool is used to remove the rear cogs on a freehub.

chase, wild goose: (see "goose".)

circlip (snapring, Jesus clip): a c-shaped snapring that fits in a groove to hold parts together.

clip-in pedal (clipless pedal): a pedal that relies on spring-loaded clips to grip the cleat on the rider's shoes, without the use of toe clips and straps.

clipless pedal: (see "clip-in pedal".)

cog: the sprockets located on the drive side of the rear hub.

compression damping: the deadening or diminishing of the speed of the compression of a spring on impact.

cone: a threaded conical nut that serves to hold a set of bearings in place and also provides a smooth surface upon which those bearings can roll.

crankarm: the lever attached at the bottom- bracket spindle used to transmit a rider's energy to the chain.

crankarm-fixing bolt: the bolt attaching the crank to the bottom-bracket spindle on a cotterless drive train.

crankset: the assembly that includes a bottom bracket, two crankarms, chainring set and accompanying nuts and bolts.

cross three: a pattern used by wheel builders, that calls for each spoke to cross three others in its path from the hub to the rim.

cup: a cup-shaped bearing surface that surrounds the bearings in a bottom bracket, headset or hub.

damper: a mechanism in a suspension fork or shock that provides damping of the spring's oscillation.

damping: the deadening and diminishing of the oscillation of a spring, as in a suspension fork or shock.

derailleur: a gear-changing device that allows a rider to move the chain from one cog or chainring to another while the

crankarms are in motion.

derailleur hanger: a metal extension of the right rear dropout through which the rear derailleur is mounted to the frame.

diamond frame: the traditional bicycle frame shape.

dish: a difference in spoke tension on the two sides of the rear wheel so that the wheel is centered over the hub.

disc brake: a brake that stops the bike by squeezing brake pads against a circular disc attached to the wheel.

double: a two-chainring drivetrain setup (as opposed to a three-chainring, or "triple", one).

down tube: the tube that connects the head tube and bottom-bracket shell.

drivetrain: the crankarms, chainrings, bottom bracket, front derailleur, chain, rear derailleur and freewheel (or cassette).

drop: the perpendicular distance between a horizontal line passing through the wheel hub centers and the center of the bottom bracket.

dropouts: the slots in the forks and rear triangle where the wheel axles attach.

dust cap: a protective cap keeping dirt away from a part.

elastomer: a urethane spring used in suspension forks and swing arms.

ferrule: a cap for the end of cable housing.

fixed cup: the non-adjustable cup of the bottom bracket located on the drive side of the bottom bracket.

flange: the largest diameter of the hub

where the spoke heads are anchored.

fork: the part that attaches the front wheel to the frame.

fork crown: the cross piece connecting the fork legs to the steering tube.

fork ends: (see "dropouts".)

fork rake (rake): the perpendicular offset distance of the front axle from an imaginary extension of the steering tube centerline (steering axis).

fork tips (fork ends): (see "dropouts".)

frame: the central structure of a bicycle to which all of the parts are attached.

freewheel: a removable cluster of cogs that allows a rider to stop pedaling as the bicycle is moving forward.

friction shifter: a traditional (non-indexed) shifter attached to the frame or handle bars. Cable tension is maintained by a combination of friction washers and bolts.

front triangle (main triangle): the head tube, top tube, down tube and seat tube of a bike frame.

"girl's" bike: (see "step-through frame".)

goose chase, wild: (see "wild".)

Grip Shift: a shifter that is integrated with the handlebar grip of a mountain bike. The rider shifts gears by twisting the grip. (see also "twist shifter".)

hex key: (see "Allen key".)

headset: the cup, lock ring, and bearings that hold the fork to the frame and allow the fork to turn in the frame.

head tube: the front tube of the frame through which the steering tube of the fork

passes. The head tube is attached to the top tube and down tube and locates the headset.

hub: the central part of a wheel to which the spokes are anchored and through which the wheel axle passes.

hub brake: a disc, drum or coaster brake that stops the wheel with friction applied to a braking surface attached to the hub.

hydraulic brake: a type of brake that uses oil pressure to move the brake pads against the braking surface.

index shifter: a shifter that clicks into fixed positions as it moves the derailleur from gear to gear.

inner wire: see "cable".

Jesus clip: (see "circlip.")

jockey wheel or jockey pulley: a circular cog-shaped-pulley attached to the rear derailleur used to guide, apply tension to and laterally move the chain from rear cog to rear cog.

knobby tire: an all-terrain tire used on mountain bikes.

link: (1) a pivoting steel hook on a V-brake arm that the cable-guide "noodle" hooks into. (2) (see "chain link".)

locknut: a nut that serves to hold the bearing adjustment in a headset, hub or pedal.

lockring: the outer ring that tightens the adjustable cup of a bottom bracket against the face of the bottom-bracket shell.

lock washer: a notched or toothed washer that serves to hold surrounding nuts and washers in position.

master link: a detachable link that holds the chain together. The master link can be opened by hand without a chain tool.

mixte frame: (see "step-through frame".)

mounting bolt: a bolt that mounts a part to a frame, fork, or component. (see also "pivot bolt.")

needle bearing: steel cylindrical cartridge with rod-shaped rollers arranged coaxially around the inside walls

noodle: curved cable-guide pipe on a V-brake arm which stops the cable housing and directs the cable to the cable anchor bolt on the opposite arm.

nipple: a small nut specially designed to receive the end of a spoke and fit the holes of a rim.

outer wire: (see "cable housing".)

outer wire stop: (see "cable stop".)

pin spanner: a V-shaped wrench with two tip-end pins that is used for tightening the adjustable cup of the bottom bracket.

pivot bolt: a fixing bolt that fastens the brake arm to the frame or fork.

preload: (see spring preload)

Presta valve: thin, metal tire valve that uses a locking nut to stop air flow from the tire.

quick release: (1) the tightening lever and shaft used to attach a wheel to the fork or rear dropouts without using axle nuts. (2) a quick-opening lever and shaft pinching the seatpost inside the seat tube, in lieu of a wrench-operated bolt. (3) a quick cable release on a brake. (4) a fixing mechanism that can be quickly opened and closed, as on a brake cable or wheel axle. (5) a fixing bolt that can be quickly opened and closed by a lever.

quill: the vertical tube of a stem that

inserts into the fork steering tube. It has an expander wedge and bolt inside to secure the stem to the steering tube.

race: a ring-shaped surface on which the bearings roll freely.

Rapid-fire shifter: an indexing shifter manufactured by Shimano for use on mountain bikes with two separate levers operating each shift cable.

rear triangle: the rear portion of the bicycle frame, including the seatstays, the chainstays and the seat tube.

rebound damping: the diminishing of speed of return of a spring after compression.

rim: the outer hoop of a wheel to which the tire is attached.

roller-cam brakes: a brake system using pulleys and a cam to force the brake pads against the rim surface.

saddle (seat): a platform made of leather and/or plastic upon which the rider sits.

Schrader valve: a high-pressure air valve with a spring-loaded air-release pin inside. Schrader valves are found on bicycle tubes and air-sprung suspension forks as well as on adjustable rear shocks and automobile tires and tubes.

sealed bearing: a bearing enclosed in an attempt to keep contaminants out. (see also "cartridge bearing".)

seat cluster: the intersection of the seat tube, top tube, and seat stays.

seat: (see "saddle.")

seatpost: the post to which the saddle is

secured.

skewer: a hub quick release or a shaft passing through a stack of elastomer bumpers in a suspension fork.

snapring: (see "circlip.")

spider: a star-shaped piece of metal that connects the right crank arm to the chainrings.

spokes: metal rods that connect the hub to the rim of a wheel.

spring: an elastic contrivance, which, when compressed, returns to its original shape by virtue of its elasticity. In bicycle suspension applications, the spring used is normally either an elastic polymer cylinder, a coil of steel or titanium wire, or compressed air.

spring preload: the initial loading of a spring so part of its compression range is taken up prior to impact.

sprocket: a circular, multiple-toothed piece of metal that engages a chain. (See also: cog and chainring.)

standover clearance ("standover height"): the distance between the top tube of the bike and the rider's crotch when standing over the bicycle.

star nut ("Star-fangled nut"): a tanged nut that is forced down onto the steering tube and anchors the stem bolt of a threadless headset.

steering axis: the imaginary line about which the fork rotates.

steering tube: the vertical tube on a fork that is attached to the fork crown and fits inside the head tube.

step-through frame ("women's frame"; "girl's bike"; "mixte frame"): a bicycle frame with a steeply up-angled top tube connecting the bottom of the seat tube to the top of the head tube. The frame design is intended to provide ease of stepping over the frame and ample standover clearance.

straddle cable: short segment of cable connecting two brake arms together.

straddle-cable holder: (see "yoke.")

swingarm: the movable rear end of a rear-suspension frame.

threadless headset: (see "AheadSet".)

three cross: (see "cross three".)

thumb shifter: a thumb-operated shift lever attached on top of the handlebars.

top tube: the tube that connects to the seat tube to the head tube.

triple: a term used to describe the three-chainring combination attached to the right crankarm.

twist shifter: a cable-pulling derailleur control handle surrounding the handlebar adjacent to the hand grip; it is twisted forward or back to cause the derailleur to shift. (see also "Grip Shift.")

U-brake: a mountain-bike brake consisting of two arms shaped like inverted L's affixed to posts on the frame or fork.

V-brake: a cable-operated rim brake consisting of two vertical brake arms with a cable link and cable guide pipe on one arm and a cable anchor on the opposite arm.

wheel base: the horizontal distance between the two wheel axles.

wild goose chase: (see "chase.")

women's frame: (see "step-through frame.)

yoke: the part attaching the brake cable to the straddle cable on a cantilever or U-brake.